Understanding
Child Development

Join us on the web at

EarlyChildEd.delmar.com

Understanding
Child Development

Sheila Anderson

THOMSON

™

DELMAR LEARNING

Australia • Canada • Mexico • Singapore • Spain • United Kingdom • United States

Printed in Canada
1 2 3 4 5 XXX 11 10 09 08 07

For more information contact Thomson Delmar Learning, Executive Woods, 5 Maxwell Drive, Clifton Park, NY 12065-2919

Or find us on the World Wide Web at http://www.delmarlearning.com, or www.earlychilded.delmar.com

ISBN-13: 978-1-4180-3816-8
ISBN-10: 1-4180-3816-4

Library of Congress Cataloging-in-Publication Data

Anderson, Sheila.
  Understanding Child Development/Sheila Anderson.
      p. cm.
  Includes bibliographical references.
  ISBN 1-4180-3816-4
  1. Early childhood education. 2. Early childhood teachers—In-service training.
  3. Child development. I. Title.
  LB1139.23.A53 2008
  372.21—dc22
                                                          2007007315

NOTICE TO THE READER
The authors and Thomson Delmar Learning affirm that the Web site URLs referenced herein were accurate at the time of printing. However, due to the fluid nature of the Internet, we cannot guarantee their accuracy for the life of the edition.

TABLE OF CONTENTS

This tool was developed to help you, the budding teacher and/or child care provider, as you move into your first classroom. The editors at Thomson Delmar Learning encourage and appreciate your feedback on this or any of our other products. Go to http://www.earlychilded. delmar.com and click on the "Professional Enhancement series feedback" link to let us know what you think.

INTRODUCTION

Throughout a college program of preparation to become an early childhood educator, students take many courses and read many textbooks. Their knowledge grows as they accumulate ideas from lectures, readings, experiences, and discussions. When they finish their coursework, graduate, and move into their first teaching positions, students often leave behind some of the books they have used. The hope is, however, that they will take with them the important ideas from their classes and books as they begin their own professional practice.

More experienced colleagues or mentors sometimes support teachers in their first teaching positions, helping them make the transition between college classroom and being responsible for a group of young children. Other times, new teachers are left to travel their own paths, relying on their own resources. Whatever your situation, this professional enhancement guide is designed to provide reminders of what you have learned, as well as resources to help you make sense of and apply that knowledge.

Teachers of young children are under great pressure today. From families, there are the demands for support in their difficult tasks of child-rearing in today's fast-paced and changing world. Some families become so overwhelmed with the tasks of parenting that they seem to leave too much responsibility on the shoulders of teachers and caregivers. From administrators and institutions, there are expectations that sometimes seem overwhelming. Teachers are being held accountable for children's learning in ways unprecedented in even the recent past. Public scrutiny has led to insistence on teaching practices that may seem contrary to the best interests of children or their teachers. New teachers may find themselves caught between the realities of the schools or centers where they are employed and their own philosophies and ideals of working with children. When faced with such dilemmas, it is important for these individuals to be able to fall back and reflect on what they know of best practices, renewing their professional determination to make appropriate decisions for children.

This professional enhancement guide provides the following tools for such reflection:

- journal ideas
- review of the National Association for the Education of Young Children (NAEYC) Code of Ethical Conduct
- key ideas about developmentally appropriate practice, the process of decision making that allows teachers to provide optimum environments for children from birth through age eight
- information about typical developmental patterns of children from birth through school age
- practices for supporting the development of children from infancy through age eight
- suggestions for working with children with special needs and diverse families
- tools to assist teachers in gathering data through observation and assessment that can be used to set appropriate goals for individual children
- tools for evaluating teaching practices and setting goals
- guides for planning appropriate classroom experiences and resources for professional development
- descriptions of other resources available for teachers and educators
- insight into issues and trends facing early childhood educators today

Becoming a teacher is a process of continuing to grow, learn, reflect, and discover through experience. Having these resources may help you along your way. Good luck on your journey!

REFLECTIONS FOR GROWING TEACHERS

Development refers to the complex, dynamic changes that occur throughout the lifespan. As a teacher, one of your roles is to be familiar with how children develop, grow, and learn. You will have the responsibility of providing them with the resources and experiences needed to optimize development. Your ability to do this is based firmly on your knowledge of child development. Through your interactions with young children and their families, you can further your knowledge of both individual development and universal developmental patterns.

Teachers spend most of their time working with young children and families. During the day, questions and concerns arise and decisions must be made, meaning teachers must always be reflective about their work. You may feel too busy to spend time reflecting, but experienced professional teachers have learned that reflection sustains their best work. It is important to regularly take time to consider the questions and concerns that arise from your work with young children. Some teachers use journals to document events, clarify problems, and record professional insights.

Keeping a child development journal can help you gain a better understanding of development and resolve problems you encounter in the classroom. A child development journal is a daily (or weekly) record of your activities and reactions regarding children. To get started, think about your own childhood, then begin your journal with the following reflections:

1. Record your earliest childhood memory, then consider: What made it memorable? Has it had a lasting effect on your development? If so, how?

2. Describe a significant relationship during your childhood that felt supportive. Make a note of the specific things the other person said and did. How has it influenced your development?

3. Describe an experience in your childhood where you felt important and valued. Include how this value was communicated to you (e.g., affection, hugs, words of appreciation, etc.), who communicated it, and how it has impacted your development.

4. Record an experience with peers from your childhood. Evaluate the impact peer experiences have had on your social and emotional development.

5. Record a learning experience that you enjoyed and one that was difficult. Analyze the specific factors that contributed to your enjoyment or difficulty.

6. Articulate your own philosophy of child development. Include your thoughts about theories of development, factors that influence development (both those that promote and those that inhibit), the role of culture and context in development and identify basic human needs.

7. Write your definition of "family." Include what you think constitutes a family and the role of families in education.

Each day as you work with children, make a mental note of experiences and your reactions. After work, record those experiences that you feel have importance and reflect on changes or inconsistencies in your reactions and beliefs (Charlesworth, 2008). Reflection is one of the most powerful strategies to change personal behaviors and improve professional practices. Finding time to examine you own thoughts, feelings, and beliefs both alone and with others will relieve stress and improve your life. Care for yourself so you will have the resources needed to care for others.

CODE OF ETHICAL CONDUCT

As an early childhood professional, you will be required to make decisions that impact the development of children and families on a daily basis. Many times these decisions are complex and involve ethical concerns. The National Association for the Education of Young Children (NAEYC) has developed a Code of Ethical Conduct (NAEYC, 2005a) for early childhood professionals. The Code of Ethical Conduct was created as a guide for resolving ethical dilemmas. A full copy of the Code of Ethical Conduct may be obtained from the NAEYC Web site (see "Recommended Web Site" section). The Code of Ethical Conduct is based on the following core values:

1. Childhood is a unique and important stage in the life cycle.

2. Knowledge of child development is the foundation for work with children.

3. Close relationships between families and children must be recognized and supported.

4. The uniqueness, dignity, and worth of each individual child, family member, and colleague must be respected.

5. Children are best understood when considering the contexts of family, culture, and society.

6. Children and adults should be fully supported in acquiring their full potential through relationships based on trust, respect, and positive regard.

The Code of Ethical Conduct addresses ethical concerns for early childhood professionals arising in four areas:

- children
- families

- colleagues

- society

The following section will briefly review the principles governing ethical conduct that are most closely linked to child development—those in the areas of children and families (the areas of colleagues and society are also critical and will be beneficial to review on your own). Within each area—children, family, colleagues, and society—ideals and aspirations for professionals are identified and principles or guidelines that apply to decision making are given. The foremost principle of the Code of Ethical Conduct states: "Above all, we shall not harm children. We shall not participate in practices that are disrespectful, degrading, dangerous, exploitative, intimidating, emotionally damaging, or physically harmful" (NAEYC, 2005a, p. 3). Your first responsibility as a professional is to protect children from harm of any type. Other responsibilities to children include the following:

- Avoid discriminatory practices based on race, ethnicity, religion, gender, national origin, language, ability, behavior, or beliefs of parents.

- Include staff, parents, and other professionals (mental health, health care, special education, etc.) with relevant knowledge in the decision-making process concerning a child.

- Maximize the potential of each child by adapting teaching strategies, the learning environment, and the curriculum, and by consulting with specialists and the child's family. When efforts to work with the child and family continue to result in the child not benefiting from the program your responsibility is to provide the family with recommendations and assistance in finding appropriate services that can meet the child's needs.

- Know and follow local laws for protecting children from abuse (physical, verbal, sexual, and emotional) and neglect. This includes reporting suspected abuse to community agencies, following up to ensure appropriate action was taken, and, when appropriate, informing parents or guardian's of the action that has been taken. When child protective agency services are not effective, your responsibility is to advocate for improvement of those services.

- If you become aware of a situation or practice that is harmful to children, inform those with authority to correct the problem and protect children from unsafe situations.

The second area of the Code of Ethical Conduct (NAEYC, 2005a) discusses the primary importance of families in children's development. Early childhood professionals and families share a common interest in the healthy development of children. You will be primarily responsible for building the collaboration between home and child care or school settings that enhance's the development of children (see also "Supporting Diverse Families" section). Principles guiding this process include the following:

- Always allow family members access to their child's classroom or program.

- Give families information about the program's philosophy and policies, personnel qualifications, teaching and learning, child development, accidents, risk of contagious illness or disease, and emotional stress the child is exposed to.

- When appropriate, involve families in decision making about program policies.

- Involve families in all significant decisions concerning their children.

- Inform families if their child is involved in an accident or exposed to inherent health risks, including contagious diseases and emotional stress.

- Inform families if their child is participating in research of any type through your program, and give them the opportunity to withdraw. Do not permit research that may hinder the development of children.

- Do not exploit families for the gain of program personnel.

- Avoid any relationship with a family member that would compromise your effectiveness with children.

- Maintain confidentiality and respect the right of families to privacy. This includes establishing and maintaining formal written confidentiality policies. Do not disclose confidential information about a family or intrude into their lives, unless a child's welfare is at risk.

- When family members are in disagreement, you have a responsibility to work openly with them, by sharing observations, providing accurate information and refraining from advocating for one party over another.

- Know the community resources and professional services that support families in your local area. Make referrals for families as needed and then follow up to ensure that needs have been provided for.

Applying the principles outlined in the Code of Ethical Conduct will help you develop confidence in your own decisions. As you adhere to the Code of Ethical Conduct, children, parents, and colleagues will recognize your professionalism and find it easier to develop trusting, constructive relationship's with you.

CASE STUDIES

Many daily decisions happen rather quickly. Taking time to consider how you will handle problems before they arise will help you respond effectively under challenging circumstances. The following case studies are based on actual classroom experience. To increase your familiarity with ethical principles, obtain a full copy of the NAEYC Code of Ethical Conduct (see "Recommended Web Site" section) and then consider which ideals and principles would be applicable in each scenario.

1. Three-year-old Spencer was adopted by a wealthy older couple when he was 18 months old. He had been removed from his birth mother by the state due to neglect. He displays some symptoms of fetal alcohol syndrome. He seems well cared for and attached to his new family. While you are visiting with his mother during a parent activity, she expresses frustration with attempts to help Spencer develop independent toileting. "We just don't know what to do. He doesn't seem to get it," she explains in frustration. "My husband has even tried rubbing his nose in the poop, like you would with a dog, and still he doesn't get it!" *How should you react? Is this maltreatment?*

2. During a staff meeting the director asks if anyone has any concerns. One of your colleagues says that he is concerned that

many teachers are using food for art and sensory activities. He believes this is unethical as it teaches children to play with their food, and because it is disrespectful when so many children in the world go hungry. Another staff member brings up the point that children are allowed to play with water, yet it is in short supply throughout much of the world and vital to sustaining life. *What do you think? How does this relate to ethics?*

3. You are teaching kindergarten. Your assistant, Kelly, has been providing after-school child care for a single father of one of the children in your class. After several weeks of working for this family she discloses that their relationship has become physically intimate. *What counsel would you give her? What are your ethical responsibilities?*

4. One of the toddlers in your class is struggling with biting. You have tried several interventions, and are noticing gradual improvement. However, several parents of other children are now threatening to leave the program if the biting toddler is not removed from the class. *What are your ethical responsibilities? How would you respond?*

5. One afternoon while you are helping some of the children at the sensory table, two-year-old Courtney slips out the door. A few minutes later a woman passing by finds her and returns her to the classroom. You had not noticed she was gone. You're surprised and embarrassed. *Who should be informed about what happened? What are your ethical responsibilities?*

RECOMMENDED WEB SITE

National Association for the Education of Young Children. (2005). *Code of ethical conduct* (Rev. ed.). Washington, DC: Author. Available online at http://www.naeyc.org.

DEVELOPMENTALLY APPROPRIATE PRACTICE

As an early childhood professional you will have the opportunity to promote and establish high-quality programs for young children. You will encounter a variety of opinions from colleagues, administrators, and families about how to accomplish this. To complicate matters further, children are constantly changing as they develop. You may find yourself feeling unsure about what is best for children. The NAEYC's 1996 position statement "Developmentally Appropriate Practice in Early Childhood Programs Serving Children from Birth through Age 8" (see "Recommended Web Site" section), helps clarify these questions by providing guidelines on how to apply your knowledge of child development in the classroom.

Copple and Bredekamp (2006) explain that developmentally appropriate practice (DAP) means purposefully deciding when, what, and how to teach children by considering their age, experience, interests and abilities, and the social and cultural context in which they live. Similar to the Code of Ethical Conduct, DAP guidelines are based on principles. The NAEYC (1996) outlines 12 principles of development to guide the decisions of early childhood professionals. For the purpose of this review, some of these principles have been synthesized into five basic ideas.

1. Development takes place in a relatively orderly sequence with later development building on earlier development. This means that predictable, universal patterns of change and growth are evident and occur across all domains (physical, social-emotional, cognitive, language, motor). For example, most infants first learn to roll over, then sit, crawl, and finally walk. You may recall that theorists such as Erikson and Piaget have outlined predictable, universal stages of development based on this principle.

Development is also predictable in the sense that it will proceed toward greater complexity, organization, and internalization. For example, infants make vocalizations, then attach meaning to sounds and gestures; older children learn how to use words to represent meaning, then symbols and writing to express their inner thoughts. Because development is moving toward greater complexity, both positive and negative early experiences will impact future development.

There are times during development that specific types of learning and development occur most efficiently (e.g., vision coordination in the first few months of life; language development in the early years). Negative impacts such as delays in language can be overcome later, but it is more difficult. Early experience may also affect later development in a cumulative manner, meaning that frequent experiences have a greater and longer-lasting impact than occasional experiences. For example, an infant whose cries are not attended to most of the time may have greater difficulty developing a sense of trust and security, as compared to the infant whose cries are consistently responded to. Early experiences may also have delayed effects. For example, offering children extrinsic rewards such as stickers or toys, may immediately increase a desired behavior; however, continued use of extrinsic rewards may decrease long-term internal motivation.

Due to these universal similarities, teachers can make predictions about what will appropriately support the learning and development of children. Your knowledge of the universal sequence of development across domains provides a framework for planning, preparing learning environments, solving behavioral difficulties, setting goals for children, and educating families. However, keep in mind that variety exists in how these changes are manifest and the meaning cultures place upon them. For example, as toddlers become more independent, this independence is encouraged by some cultures and discouraged by others. The cultural context influences how toddlers explore and regulate their need for independence. In the following sections, charts of developmental characteristics for each domain give specific information regarding predictable universal development. Developmental alerts are also provided and can help identify the need for intervention.

2. Development in one domain influences development in other domains. This means that the physical, motor, cognitive, language, and social-emotional domains are all interrelated, and development or lack of development in one domain can enhance or limit development in the other domains. A problem with physical growth such as malnutrition will probably cause delay in cognitive functioning, motor skills, language, and social-emotional development. Likewise, well-nourished children are more likely to have development proceed as expected across domains. When planning curriculum, attend to these connections. For example, an infant's cognitive and language development is facilitated through increasing motor skills, healthy social relationships, and consistent physical growth.

3. Development occurs at individual rates and varies across domains. Not only is development universal and orderly, it is also varied and unique. Variations are influenced by the complex and dynamic interactions of genetic inheritance, biological maturation, physical environment, and social context. These factors begin to work from the moment of conception and ensure that each child will be a unique individual with personality, temperament, and learning characteristics like no other. Individual children develop preferred ways of learning, representation, and expression. Rigid expectations of compliance to group norms are contrary to the need for individual development and neglect consideration of cultural context. Expecting and valuing individual differences helps adults individualize curriculum and interactions with children and families. An individualized curriculum constructed from the interests and needs of children enhances motivation and facilitates development.

4. Development is maximized within a context where basic needs are met. All human beings have basic needs, including the following:

- The need for security and safety: Children need to feel a sense of predictability, safety, and dependability concerning both physical and psychological needs. These needs are met when basic food, clothing, medical care, mental health care, and supervision are provided. The child is also protected from unsafe situations. Emotional safety is provided and the child feels valued.

- The need for love, acceptance, and respect: Children need love and affection from significant adults who are consistently a part of their lives. They need to be understood, appreciated, and accepted for their unique attributes.

■ The need for competency: Children are learning to regulate their own behavior and function independently in the world. They need information, skills, and guidance that will help them develop responsibility for their own actions, as well as the skills and abilities that will allow them to accomplish their goals and function productively in society.

5. Play facilitates development through opportunities to actively construct knowledge, practice current skills, and experience challenge. Children are actively engaged in constructing knowledge; they are not merely passive recipients. The types of knowledge they are constructing include motor, cognitive, language, social, emotional, and cultural understandings. They need many opportunities to explore, practice, and integrate these emerging skills. Play is usually open-ended and flexible, which limits the chances of failure and maximizes choices. Play affords children opportunities to simultaneously try on roles, confront challenges, and practice self-regulation. Play is especially important in facilitating social negotiation skills, imagination, and symbolic representation. Through play you can provide opportunities for children to practice current skills and meet goals that are reachable, yet challenging. To identify what makes something challenging yet achievable, the following should be considered:

■ children's previous experience

■ developmental readiness

■ knowledge and skills

■ context for learning

To guide your application of developmental principles, Copple and Bredekamp (2006) suggest three questions to ask when making decisions about teaching young children:

■ **Is it age-appropriate?** Many developmental characteristics are predictable and are related to the age of children. Knowing the sequence of development and usual age characteristics will help you identify general needs and expectations, plan room arrangement, choose toys, plan group activities, start assessments, and make a schedule.

■ **Is individually appropriate?** Consider all that makes an individual child unique. This includes development, preferences, background, learning style, and special needs. Knowing these characteristics will help you fine-tune your instruction by identifying what motivates individual children, what they are ready to learn, and how they prefer to learn. Some children will be developing faster or more slowly than the norm. Your practices should be adapted to reflect this.

- **Is it culturally and socially appropriate for the context in which the children live?** From the moment of birth children learn about expectations, values, and appropriate behavior from their families. Cultural rules about personal space, courtesy, eye contact, dress, reactions to emotions, and many other aspects of life are firmly developed very early. Culture is a dynamic component of a child's individuality. Teachers are responsible for ensuring that each child feels a sense of belonging and acceptance within the classroom. In order to accomplish this you will need to welcome families into your classroom, develop a mutually trusting relationship, involve them in decisions about children, and establish consistent communication routines.

Essentially, DAP is a tool that enables teachers to translate what they know about child development into classroom actions (see Table 1–1). DAP occurs when teachers are perceptive of children's needs and adapt teaching practices to meet those needs. Even seasoned teachers find themselves regularly reflecting upon daily experiences and seeking to better understand children and improve their teaching practices. The NAEYC (1996) organized five guidelines to help teachers apply DAP to specific areas of teaching. These guidelines are: (see "Guidelines for Developmentally Appropriate Practice" section):

- Create a caring community of learners.

- Teach to enhance learning and development.

- Construct appropriate curriculum.

- Assess children's learning and development.

- Establish reciprocal relationships with families.

The material presented here is only a brief review of the general principles governing development and DAP decision making. You are encouraged to obtain the full copy of these guidelines and recommendations for your own reference (see "Recommended

TABLE 1–1   EXAMPLES OF DEVELOPMENTALLY APPROPRIATE DECISIONS

What teachers know about child development	What teachers do in the classroom
	Teachers treat children with dignity and respect by . . .
Young children need warm, responsive relationships.	listening to comments.
	responding quickly and consistently to needs.
	learning about the individual needs and interests of children.
	providing children with opportunities to play and work cooperatively.
	establishing reciprocal relationships with families.
	providing an organized environment and orderly routine.
	Teachers provide children with . . .
Young children need hands-on, minds-on, individualized learning activities.	sufficient time to explore child-initiated activities.
	concrete activities that allow exploration and experimentation with objects.
	a wide variety of materials and equipment.
	opportunities to collaborate with adults and peers.
	guidance and direction by using strategies such as open-ended questions that extend thinking.
	Teachers plan curriculum by . . . .
Young children need experiences that are meaningful (related to previous experiences).	starting with ideas that interest children and building upon children's current knowledge and abilities.
	allowing the interests and questions of children to guide the investigation of a concept.
	connecting the cultures of families to classroom experiences.
	including a broad range of content integrated across disciplines.
	choosing activities that are socially relevant, intellectually engaging, and personally meaningful.

Source: Adapted from "Position Statement. Developmentally Appropriate Practice in Early Childhood Programs Serving Children from Birth through Age 8," NAEYC, 1996. Washington, DC: Author. Available online at http://www.naeyc.org/about/positions/pdf/ PSDAP98.PDF

Web Site" section). The next sections provide further information on observation and assessment, planning, and adapting your teaching practices in developmentally appropriate ways to meet the needs of children and families, but before you move on, take a moment to consider the following case studies.

CASE STUDIES

1. Some children in your preschool class for four-year-olds find a dead baby bird on the playground. They express concern and wonder where it came from and why it is dead. *How do you respond? What is your rationale based on the developmental characteristics of four-year-olds?*

2. You are conducting parent-teacher conferences for your kindergarten class. One of the mothers shows you a dot-to-dot activity her son brought home from school a few weeks ago. You had used the dot-to-dot as a math center activity with the objective of providing practice in sequencing numbers. The mother expresses concern that this is a "worksheet" and is not developmentally appropriate. *Is the worksheet developmentally appropriate? What is your rationale? How would you respond?*

3. Several infants in your class are experiencing increased separation anxiety. Your team teacher is uncomfortable with their distress and is counseling parents to sneak out of the classroom while she distracts the infants. *Is this developmentally appropriate? What is your rationale? How would you respond to your colleague? How would you respond to parents?*

4. You have developed a curriculum theme around the story of Goldilocks and the three bears in your preschool classroom for three-year-olds. Your curriculum book provides a pattern for dramatic play masks that children can cut, color, and use to act out the story. Your director has a strict policy against making copies for preschool art projects. You are sure she will not let you make the copies at school or approve of the activity. *Is the director's policy developmentally appropriate? What is your rationale? Could this activity be adapted to better facilitate the development of young children?*

5. While observing your class at lunch, you notice the lunch aide working with one of the immigrant children in your class. This child has been in the United States less than a year and is fluent in her primary language. She seems to enjoy school, but rarely speaks. She is gesturing to the lunch aide that she would like more yogurt. The lunch aide is refusing to give her the food until she says "yogurt." *Is this developmentally appropriate? What is your rationale? How would you respond?*

6. It's Halloween in your first-grade classroom, and a school-wide party with a costume parade is planned for the day. Sari

arrives and looks around nervously. She watches the other children intently discussing and sharing their costume ideas. You notice that she doesn't seem to have an extra bag with a costume. You ask, "Did you forget your costume?" She shakes her head and looks down. "I don't have one," she answers. You are not really sure how to respond, but suggest, "I'll help you make one during art time." Sari begins to cry and says, "No, my family doesn't celebrate Halloween." *How will you respond? Include responses to Sari, her parents, and the school principal.*

RECOMMENDED READING

Copple, C., & Bredekamp, S. (2006). *Basics of developmentally appropriate practices.* Washington, DC: National Association for the Education of Young Children.

RECOMMENDED WEB SITE

National Association for the Education of Young Children. (1996). *Position statement. Developmentally appropriate practice in early childhood programs serving children from birth through age 8.* Washington, DC: Author. Available online at http://www.naeyc.org.

GUIDELINES FOR DEVELOPMENTALLY APPROPRIATE PRACTICE

The NAEYC's DAP guidelines can be implemented in your daily work with children in the following ways:

- **Create a caring environment among children and adults.**
  Children:
    - learn personal responsibility.
    - develop constructive relationships with others.
    - respect individual and cultural differences.

  Adults:
    - get to know each child, taking into account individual differences and developmental level.
    - adjust the pace and content of the curriculum so that children can be successful most of the time.
    - bring each child's culture and language into the setting, welcoming their families.
    - expect children to be tolerant of others' differences.

- **Develop a curriculum and schedule that will allow children to select and initiate their own activities.**
  Children:
    - learn through active involvement in a variety of learning experiences.
    - build independence by taking on increasing responsibilities.
    - initiate their own activities to follow their interests.

  Adults:
    - provide a variety of materials and activities that are concrete and real.
    - provide a variety of work places and spaces.

- arrange the environment so that children can work alone or in groups.
- extend children's learning by posing problems and asking thought-provoking questions.
- add complexity to tasks as needed.
- model, demonstrate, and provide information so that children can progress in their learning.

■ **Organize and integrate the program so that children develop a deeper understanding of key concepts and skills.**
Children:
- engage in activities that reflect their current interests.
- plan and predict outcomes of their research.
- share information and knowledge with others.

Adults:
- plan related activities and experiences that broaden children's knowledge and skills.
- design curriculum to foster important skills such as literacy and numeracy.
- adapt instruction for children who are ahead of or behind age-appropriate expectations.
- plan curriculum so that children achieve important developmental goals.

■ **Provide activities and experiences that help children develop a positive self-image within a democratic community.**
Children:
- learn through reading books about other cultures.
- read about current events and discuss how these relate to different cultures.
- accept differences among their peers, including children with disabilities.

Adults:
- provide culturally sensitive and nonsexist activities and materials that foster children's self-identity.
- design the learning environment so that children can learn new skills while using their native language.
- allow children to demonstrate their learning using their own language.
- facilitate discussion and problem solving among children.

- **Provide activities and experiences that develop children's awareness of the importance of community involvement.**

Children:

- are ready and eager to learn about the world outside their immediate environment.
- are open to considering different ways of thinking or doing things.
- can benefit from contact with others outside their homes or child care settings.

Adults:

- encourage awareness of the community at large, as well as a sense of the classroom community.
- plan experiences in facilities within the community.
- bring outside resources and volunteers into the child care setting.
- encourage children to plan their involvement based on their own interests.

OBSERVATION

No doubt your college practicum experience taught you the logistics of observing: using objective descriptions and recording specific, dated, brief, and factual information. Observation can take many forms, including the following:

- anecdotal records

- running records

- checklists

- time and event sampling

ANECDOTAL RECORD

Anecdotal records are brief notes kept by the teacher while the child is performing a task. At first this may seem daunting, but it will become a natural part of your everyday routine. Keep a small spiral notebook and pen or pencil in your pocket. When a child begins an activity, watch what the child does and write down three or four things that you actually observe the child doing. Remember to record just the facts and only the facts. For example:

10-month-old Libby pulls herself to a standing position using the toy shelf. She lets go of the shelf and stands for three seconds, then sits down. She looks at mother and smiles.

As time permits, probably during nap time, the brief notes are turned into a full scenario that can be read and understood at a later date (see Table 1–2).

Sample Anecdotal Record

Child's Name: José Observer's Name: Maria			Age: 4 yr. 5 mo. Date: April 27, 2006	
What actually happened/What I saw	**Developmental interpretation** **(Select 1 or 2 of the following)**			
José works intently as he manipulates the clay. He uses the clay tools to change the shape, contour, and texture of the clay. Occasionally he speaks quietly to himself, as if thinking aloud: "I need a little more clay right here." He continues for 15 minutes, then puts the project on the shelf for the day.	Interest in learning	X	Self-esteem/self-concept	
	Cultural acceptance		Problem solving	X
	Interest in real-life mathematical concepts		Interactions with adults	
	Literacy		Interactions with peers	
	Language expression/comprehension		Self-regulation	X
	Safe/healthy behavior		Self-help skills	
	Gross motor skills		Fine motor skills	X

TABLE 1–2 ANECDOTAL RECORD				
Child's Name: _____ Observer's Name: _____			Date: _____	
What actually happened/What I saw	**Developmental interpretation** **(Select 1 or 2 of the following)**			
	Interest in learning		Self-esteem/self-concept	
	Cultural acceptance		Problem solving	
	Interest in real-life mathematical concepts		Interactions with adults	
	Literacy		Interactions with peers	
	Language expression/comprehension		Self-regulation	
	Safe/healthy behavior		Self-help skills	
	Gross motor skills		Fine motor skills	

RUNNING RECORD

Another form of authentic assessment is the running record. It covers a longer time span and gives more information than an anecdotal record. Often it may have a specific developmental focus, such as "social interactions." A running record will give you information about other developmental areas because of its very detailed nature. This form of observation requires the caregiver to not be involved with children for several minutes while writing the observation. You will be setting yourself apart from the children and writing continuously, in as much detail as possible. You will write what the child does and says, by herself and in interactions with other people and materials. Use objective phrases to avoid interpretative and judgmental language. Note that the format for this form of assessment has two columns. The left column is for writing the actual observations and the right column is for connecting the observations to aspects of development. Remember to date all observations so that you can notice developmental change over time.

Sample Running Record

Child's Name: Tayla	Age: 6 yr. 2 mo.
Observer's Name: Jorge	Date: April 27, 2005
Developmental Focus: Social interactions with peers	

Tayla **is jumping rope.** *Annalisa* **jumps rope next to her. Both girls repeat "Johnny and Sara sitting in the tree, K-I-S-S-I-N-G."** *Tayla* **says, "How about this one, '***Tayla* **and** *Annalisa* **jumping rope, J-U-M-P-I-N-G.'"** *Annalisa* **smiles and giggles. She misses the next jump, trips on the rope, and falls.** *Tayla* **stops, and asks, "Are you alright?" She puts her arm around** *Annalisa* **and gently rocks back and forth with her. As** *Annalisa's* **crying begins to subside,** *Tayla,* **smiling, says, "Let's go tell the teacher our new rhyme."** *Annalisa* **answers, "No, it's a stupid rhyme anyway, it made me fall."** *Tayla* **turns her head away from** *Annalisa,* **wrinkles her forehead, and frowns. "I like it,"** *Tayla* **asserts.** *Annalisa* **is quiet.** *Tayla* **watches her intently, then asks, "Do you still want to play with me? I like playing with you."** *Annalisa* **smiles and asks, "OK, can I make a rhyme now?"**	Gross motor skills Participates in cooperative activities Early literacy/expressive language Expresses empathy Communicates knowledge of growing skills Self-regulation/controls emotions Self-awareness Stands up for own rights Asks for what she needs

CHECKLIST

A checklist is often used as a means of assessment because it is one of the easiest assessment tools to use. A checklist consists of a predetermined list of clearly observable developmental criteria for which the observer indicates *yes* or *no*. The observer reads the developmental criteria and makes a checkmark if the decision is a *yes*. This form of assessment does not require additional notes to be recorded. Many teachers design their own checklists to fit the specific needs of their program. The checklist in Table 1–3 is an example of one that might be used to assess the social skills of children.

Make checklists for each center in your classroom and hang them on clipboards. When you observe the children at play in each center, check off skills by placing a date in the appropriate box.

TABLE 1–3   SOCIAL SKILLS CHECKLIST

Child's Name: _____   Age: yr. mo. _____
Observer's Name: _____

Skills	Dates
■ Desires to and can work near other children	
■ Interacts with other children	
■ Takes turns with other children	
■ Enters play with others in a positive manner	
■ Shares materials and supplies	
■ Stands up for own rights in a positive manner	
■ Forms friendships with peers	
■ Engages in positive commentary on other children's work	
■ Shows empathy	
■ Negotiates compromises with other children	
■ Demonstrates prosocial behavior	
■ Participates in cooperative group activities	
■ Resolves conflicts with adult prompts	
■ Resolves conflicts without adult prompts	

TIME AND EVENT SAMPLING

The last type of observation that a teacher should perform is a time or event sampling. These are similar in focus, but involve different steps. A *time sampling* asks the teacher to set a timer, each time the timer goes off, the teacher looks at a particular child and writes down what the child is doing. Again, only the facts are written. For example:

The timer is set to go off every 10 minutes. I will look at Ario and see what he is doing when I hear the timer. The timer goes off; I look at Ario. Ario **is working with Kayla in the dramatic play area. "I'll be the fire-fighter, you are my helper,"** *he says. The timer goes off again. Ario is* **at the easel. He is using the largest brush and yellow paint. The paper is almost completely covered with yellow paint.**

As mentioned, an *event sampling* is similar, but the teacher looks at events instead of being directed by a timer. The teacher zeros in on an event and writes down everything observed pertaining to the event.

Sample Event Sampling

Antecedent	Behavior	Consequence
Cody sits down in the chair next to him.	Hitting another child	*Teacher stops the hitting. Says "Cody is crying. He is hurt from being hit."*

Assessment and observation tasks may seem overwhelming as you begin your career in early childhood education, but do not shy away from them. Take the challenge and begin to look for the positive aspects of learning and mastering a new skill. Picture yourself as a student in your classroom and imagine what it is like to perfect something your teacher has just asked you to do. How does it make you feel? Now begin—approach your program assessment and observation tasks with confidence and sensitivity.

SUPPORTING THE DEVELOPMENT OF INFANTS

Working with infants provides an exciting opportunity to observe the processes of development. New accomplishments and developmental milestones often emerge within weeks or even days of one another. This is not only exciting, but challenging, as you will need to adapt your practices frequently. The information in this section provides suggestions to help you meet the changing needs of infants. It is organized by developmental domain, including physical, motor, cognitive, language, and social/emotional. Within each developmental domain, patterns of development are described and techniques are suggested. At the end of this section developmental alerts are identified and some considerations for working with the families of infants are provided. Let's begin with the physical growth of the infant.

PHYSICAL GROWTH

Infancy is a time of phenomenal physical growth. Physical growth proceeds in an organized manner from head to toe and from the center out. Evidence of this is seen as the infant grows; the head becomes more proportionate to the rest of the body. Most infants triple their birth weight by the end of the first year and grow approximately 1/2 to 1 inch per month. Head circumference also increases dramatically, marking significant brain growth and development (see Table 1–4). Sound health practices are imperative, as threats to physical growth can seriously delay development in other domains.

Your Role: Supporting Physical Growth
During infancy the immature systems of the body are vulnerable to illness, disease, toxins, and accidents. Sudden infant death syndrome

TABLE 1–4   CHARACTERISTICS OF INFANT PHYSICAL GROWTH

Child's Name_____   Birth Date_____

Physical Growth	Date
Birth to 1 month	
Can suck and swallow easily	
Shows continued gains in height, weight (approximately 5–6 oz per week), and head circumference	
Usually has approximately six feedings of 3–4 oz of formula or breast milk	
Does not have tears when crying	
Eyes sensitive to light	
Sees outlines and shapes; can focus on distant objects (4–30 in. away)	
Soft spots or "fontanels" are located on top and back of head	
Hearing is good; startles at sudden sounds; attentive to human voice	
Spends up to 18 hours a day sleeping (usually occurs in short periods of time, approximately 1–3 hours)	
1 to 4 months	
Weight 8–16 lb (gains approximately 0.25–0.5 lb per weak); length 20–27 in. (gains approximately 1 in. per month)	
Head circumference increases (by approximately $3/4$ in. per month at 2 months; by $5/8$ in. per month until 4 months)	
Soft spot or fontanel at back of head beginning to close	
Arms and legs of equal length, size and shape (legs may be slightly bowed)	
Feet appear flat with no arch	
Rooting and sucking reflexes are well developed	
Usually has approximately five or six feedings of 3–6 oz of formula or breast milk	
Cries with tears	
Coordinated eye movements (binocular vision)	
Spending more time awake but sleeping for longer periods, especially at night	
4 to 8 months	
Gains 1 lb per month; length increases by $1/2$ in. per month	
Head circumference increases steadily by approximately $3/8$ in. per month	
Usually has approximately five feedings of 5–8 oz of formula or breast milk and receives solid food	
Sleeps 11 to 13 hours at night; has two or three naps per day	
Begins to cut teeth (lower incisors first); drooling, biting, chewing; gums appear swollen	

(Continued)

TABLE 1—4   CHARACTERISTICS OF INFANT PHYSICAL GROWTH (*Continued*)

Physical Growth	Date
4 to 8 months	
Reflexes established: blinking, sucking, swallowing; parachute reflex appears toward the end of this stage	
Establishes true eye color	
Begins to eat some solid foods	
8 to 12 months	
Steady increases continue in height (approximately $1/_2$ in. per month) and weight (1 lb per month; triple birth weight by 12 months)	
Soft spot or fontanel in front location begins to close	
Arms and hands are more developed than feet and legs; legs may appear slightly bowed; feet are still flat	
Both eyes are coordinated—binocular coordination; points to distant objects	
Teeth: may have four upper and lower teeth, molars begin erupting	
Eats three meals per day, and snacks; may start to refuse bottle; has food likes and dislikes	
Sleeps through the night; takes at least one nap in the afternoon	

Source: Adapted from *Developmental Profiles, Pre-Birth through Twelve* (5th ed.), by K. D. Allen & L. R. Marotz, 2007, Cliffon Park, NY: Thomson Delmar Learning. Reprinted with permission of Delmar Learning, a division of Thomson Learning: http://www.thomsonrights.com. Fax 800 730-2215.

(SIDS) and respiratory problems continue to be significant contributors to infant death. Your role is to promote the healthy growth of infants by ensuring that each infant has proper nutrition and regular routines, is kept clean, and has a safe and stimulating environment in which to grow. It is also crucial to keep daily records of feeding, sleep, and elimination to monitor health and keep parents updated. The following information is a brief review of caregiver practices related to sleep patterns, feeding, diapering, and crying that promote the physical growth of infants (see Appendix A for other health practices). Some of the information may also be helpful for parent newsletters. Please keep in mind that knowledge about infants is increasing rapidly, and updates in health and safety policies are a constant necessity. Web sites and other resources are given at the end of this section to help you stay informed.

Sleep

During the first year infants are regulating their sleep patterns. Newborns sleep up to 18 hours per day, but usually for short time periods (1 to 3 hours). By the end of the first year, infants sleep approximately 12 hours a day, most of it during the night. Infants sometimes require help in developing regular sleep patterns. Consistent routines surrounding sleep help infants form a sense of security and predictability. Sleep routines and expectations should be based on the individual preferences of infants and families.

One of the main concerns with sleep during this developmental period is SIDS. The American Academy of Pediatrics (AAP) describes SIDS as the death of a seemingly healthy infant, at least two months old, while sleeping (AAP, 2005a). Placing infants on their backs to sleep and less cigarette smoking around babies has decreased dramatically the number of deaths from SIDS. The AAP recommends the following practices to further reduce the risk of SIDS.

- Place babies on their backs to sleep.

- Don't cover their heads or bundle infants when sleeping.

- Only use cribs that meet current safety standards.

If you work with infants, please be certain to provide parents with accurate information about this threat to the health of their children.

Feeding

During the first year, nutrition is based on adequate amounts of breast milk and formula. Some infants will easily develop predictable feeding schedules, while others will be variable. It is important to attend to the individual cues and unique preferences of each infant. Feeding time should be a relaxed, enjoyable routine. Young infants should be held and talked to while feeding. Older infants continue to enjoy conversations during feeding. Solid foods such as infant cereals are usually introduced around four months. Near the end of the first year, infants begin to feed themselves with finger foods and develop likes and dislikes. Marotz, Cross, and Rush (2005) recommend the following feeding procedures for infants:

- Check the temperature of warmed food before giving to infants.

- Discard leftover breast milk, formula, or partial food jars if the baby has been fed directly from the jar.

- Mix formula as directed.

- Do not warm breast milk in the microwave.

- Infant food brought from home should be in unopened containers.

- Properly sanitize feeding dishes and wash tops of jars before opening.

- Wash hands before preparing food and feeding infants.

- To prevent allergies, introduce new foods as recommended by a physician.

- Cut finger foods into bites $1/4$ in. or smaller.

- Hold and play with infants before feeding and burp them frequently, both during and after feedings.

- Pace feeding according to the cues of the infant.

Another feeding consideration is baby bottle tooth decay (BBTD), which is caused when infant teeth and gums are subjected to prolonged contact with almost any liquid other than water. This usually occurs when infants are put to bed with a bottle. However, allowing infants to suck on a bottle or breastfeed after feeding is finished, when awake or asleep, can also cause BBTD (AAP, 2005b). To prevent BBTD, the AAP recommends never putting infants to bed with a bottle, giving infants a bottle only during meals, and teaching infants to drink from a cup as soon as possible, usually by one year of age.

Crying and Colic

Babies cry to communicate their needs. When babies cry they may be communicating hunger, discomfort, need for physical contact, tiredness, boredom, or overstimulation. Quick, consistent, and appropriate responses to cries communicate to infants that the world is a safe place where their needs will be met. There are a variety of methods to soothe crying infants (see Table 1–5), but despite the best efforts of adults, frequent crying is not uncommon, especially for babies younger than three months.

Prolonged crying for unknown reasons is called colic and can be distressing for adults. Crying can be related to many factors, including time of day. Keeping a log can help you identify common factors surrounding crying episodes. Include time of day, what

TABLE 1–5 WAYS TO SOOTHE INFANTS		
Check for hunger	Swaddling	Sucking
Change diaper	Swinging or rocking	Play music
Walking or stroller	Soft talking, singing, "shh" sound	Change stimulation

Source: Adapted from "Brain Wonders 2–6 months old: Crying," Brain Wonders, (1998–2001a). Retrieved September 9, 2006, from http://www.zerotothree.org/brainwonders/caregivers. html

happened before the crying began, how long the infant cried, and why the crying stopped. Consult with parents and ask what works for them. Try to keep your practices as consistent with the practices of parents as possible. Parents may need to contact a health care provider if crying is prolonged, intense, and the infant cannot be soothed (BrainWonders, 1998–2001a).

One danger associated with crying is shaken baby syndrome, which occurs when an adult shakes an infant, usually due to anger or frustration with the infant's cries. The infant's neck muscles cannot fully support the head, causing the brain to move within the skull. This causes serious injury and death. Shaking a baby is child abuse. Shaken baby syndrome is life threatening and *immediate* medical care is needed (AAP, 2005c). You can help prevent shaken baby syndrome by educating parents and using the following coping strategies approved by the AAP when frustrated with a crying infant:

- Take a deep breath and count to 10.

- Take time out and let the infant cry alone.

- Call someone who can give you emotional support, or provide care for the infant.

- Contact a pediatrician. There may be a medical reason why the infant is crying.

Diapering
Frequent, sanitary diapering is essential in maintaining good health for infants. Your role is to change soiled diapers as soon as possible and wet diapers as needed (usually every one to three hours). Diapering should be a relaxed, individual time for infants. You may talk and sing with babies while diapering and explain what you are doing using correct terminology of body parts. The diapering surface should be near a sink with running water, and used only for

diapering. Some changing tables come with a small set of stairs to allow toddlers more independence in getting to the changing table and prevent physical injuries for adults (for hand washing procedures, see Appendix A).

Diaper rash is a relatively common problem during infancy. It usually consists of a red, bumpy rash on the diapered area. Diaper rash can be uncomfortable for infants and cause distress. The AAP (2005d) recommends preventing diaper rash by changing diapers regularly, rinsing the area with water, and applying ointment. Contact a physician if a rash develops blisters or pus-filled sores, does not go away within 48 to 72 hours, or gets worse.

MOTOR DEVELOPMENT

Infant motor development begins with reflexes. As perceptual abilities increase and the nervous system matures, voluntary control develops. This proceeds from head to toe as infants lift their head, then shoulders, and then learn to sit with support. Motor development also occurs from the center out as infants learn to control their entire arm, then hand and fingers. Near the end of the first year, motor development culminates in walking, marking the end of infancy (see Table 1–6). Though the sequence of skills is relatively predictable, each infant approaches the tasks in a unique way. Brain maturation, nutrition, sensory/motor experiences, and culture all impact how and when motor skills develop.

Your Role: Supporting Motor Development

Infants spend hours practicing motor skills in order to direct their own actions and movements. The development of motor skills gives infants a new variety of new learning opportunities, and opportunities for accidents. Your role in supporting motor skills is to create an environment that is safe, has space and materials for exploration, and encourages infants to practice emerging motor skills. Carefully arrange your classroom and choose materials that will enhance motor development and prevent mishaps by considering the guidelines presented in Table 1–7 (see p. 33).

Along with a safe, stimulating environment, encouragement, modeling, and scaffolding techniques can motivate infants to develop and practice motor skills. Each motor skill (e.g., rolling over, sitting up, crawling, etc.) can be broken down into smaller steps. For instance, to crawl infants must push themselves up, be able to support

TABLE 1–6   CHARACTERISTICS OF INFANT MOTOR DEVELOPMENT

Child's Name_____   Birth Date_____

Motor Development	Date
Birth to 1 month	
Engages in primarily reflexive motor activity—gagging, coughing, yawning, blinking, and elimination	
Displays rooting reflex when cheek is touched and startle reflex when exposed to sudden noise, touch, or quickly lowering infant	
Maintains "fetal" position, especially when sleeping	
Grasping reflex is evident as infant curls fingers around an object placed in hand	
Holds hands in a fist; does not reach for objects	
In prone position, head falls lower than the body's horizontal line, with hips flexed and arms and legs hanging down	
Turns head from side to side when lying down	
Has good upper-body muscle tone when supported under the arms	
1 to 4 months	
In prone position, Landau reflex appears and baby raises head and upper body on arms, grasping reflex disappearing	
Holds hand in open or semi-open position	
Grasps with entire hand; strength insufficient to hold items	
Movements tend to be large and jerky but are progressing toward smoother and more purposeful actions	
Turns head side to side when in a supine (face-up) position	
Increased upper-body movements: clasps hands above face, waves arms about, reaches for objects	
Begins rolling from front to back by turning head to one side and allowing trunk to follow	
Can be pulled into a sitting position and can sit with support (on lap or in infant seat) Reflexes changing: blinking established, sucking voluntary, startle reflex disappearing, parachute reflex appears (when held prone and suddenly lowered, arms are thrown out to the side)	
Uses pincer grip (finger and thumb) to pick up small objects	
Reaches for objects with both hands at the same time, later reaches with one hand	
Transfers objects from one hand to the other	
Grasps objects with entire hand	

(Continued)

TABLE 1–6   CHARACTERISTICS OF INFANT MOTOR DEVELOPMENT (*Continued*)

Motor Development	Date
4 to 8 months	
Sits alone, without support	
Pushes self to crawling position and rocks back and forth	
Rolls over back to front, front to back	
Enjoys being placed in a standing position; jumps in place	
8–12 months	
Reaches with one hand leading to grasp an offered object or toy	
Manipulates objects, transferring them from one hand to the other	
Explores new objects by poking with one finger	
Uses deliberate pincer grip to pick up small objects, toys, and finger foods	
Stacks objects; also places objects inside one another	
Releases objects by dropping or throwing; cannot intentionally put an object down	
Well balanced when sitting	
Begins pulling self to a standing position; begins to stand alone	
Creeps on hands and knees; crawls up and down stairs	
Stands by leaning on furniture; cruises by holding on to furniture and side-stepping	
Walks holding adult hand may walk alone	
Holds a cup with two hands; drinks with assistance	
Feeds self crackers, small pieces of food	

Source: Adapted from *Developmental Profiles, Pre-Birth through Twelve* (5th ed.), by K. D. Allen & L. R. Marotz, 2007. Reprinted with permission of Delmar Learning, a division of Thomson Learning: http://www.thomsonrights.com. Fax 800 730-2215.

their weight, and coordinate hand and leg movements. Individual infants approach motor skills in unique ways. Some infants enjoy rolling while others slide on their tummies, push themselves on their back, or skip crawling altogether in their excitement to walk. Watch infant cues carefully and encourage them to master skills in their own way. For examples of activities that support motor development for infants birth to one year of age, see Table 1–8 on p. 34.

Cognitive Development

During infancy senses are also becoming more refined and controlled. Perceptual and motor skills are becoming more integrated. Through movement infants are able to obtain information needed

TABLE 1–7 ROOM ARRANGEMENT CHECK LIST FOR INFANTS		
	Yes	**No**
Objects/structures with differing height for crawling and climbing—small stairs, foam mats, climbing structures, tunnels, etc.		
Toys for holding and tossing—rattles, busy boxes, lock boxes, sensory tubes, small balls, large pom-poms, etc.		
Soft items—pillows, carpet, cushions, fabric scraps of different textures, stuffed animals, etc.		
Play areas both indoors and outdoors with a variety of activities—ramps, mats, stairs, small climbers, things to push, things to crawl through, climbing mats, small staircases, etc.		
Plenty of open space for practicing motor skills, including crawling and pulling up to a standing position—carts with a handle to hold on to and push, etc.		
Music to stimulate rhythmic movement		
Activity gyms		
Things to hang above infants—wind chimes, mobiles, etc.		
Low shelves with items infants can reach—ratttles, small balls, etc.		

Source: Adapted from *Creative Resources for Infants and Toddlers,* by J. Herr & T. Swim, 1998, Albany, NY: Delmar Learning.

to begin constructing knowledge about people, objects, and things. Developmental theorist Jean Piaget believed that infant cognitive processes, like motor skills, begin with reflexes. Reflexes are infants' first interactions with the world. These interactions begin as infants occasionally come in contact with their own bodies, such as putting fingers near their mouth. As the actions are repeated they become more deliberate and infants begin to purposefully direct them. As memory develops, older infants begin to remember that an object exists, even if they cannot see it (termed *object permanence*). Soon after object permanence emerges, the infant begins to predict what will happen and tests these predictions through interactions (Piaget & Inhelder, 1969). These cognitive processes are developing during every activity and interaction the infant engages in. Observe infants closely and you will see continual examples of these advances (see Table 1–9 on p. 35).

Your Role: Supporting Cognitive Development
Infants develop cognitive abilities through play and social interactions. Your role in supporting the cognitive development of infants is to provide individual, personal interactions and a stimulating

TABLE 1–8   ACTIVITIES FOR INFANTS

Infants 1–4 Months	Infants 4–8 Months	Infants 8–12 Months
■ Be perceptive of nonmobile infants need for stimulation and move them to different areas in the room. Be sure to spend individual time holding and touching them throughout the day. ■ Put young infants on their tummies. Use a pillow to make the head slightly higher than the body. Lie near them and encourage them to lift the head by using your voice or a toy to gain their attention. ■ Help infants develop muscles and coordination by putting them on their stomachs to play for short periods of time throughout the day. ■ Put wrist or ankle bells on infants and observe if their motor action increases, becomes more coordinated, or becomes more purposeful.	■ Hold infants on your lap and support them with your arm or hand while they practice sitting. ■ Once they can sit, sit near them and roll a ball to them; encourage them to roll it back to you. ■ Build a tower with blocks, then let them knock it down. ■ As they gain control of hands and grasping, provide baskets or buckets filled with items the infant can take in and out. ■ Put a toy just out of the infant's reach and encourage the infant to get it. Provide grasping toys and show them how to jiggle the toy.	■ Continue encouraging infants to move toward object by putting objects at the edge of their reach, then verbally encouraging infants to get the objects. ■ Place infants in a standing position they enjoy. Some will like standing on your lap. ■ As infants begin cruising around furniture while holding on to it, you might offer your index fingers. Some infants enjoy holding both index fingers of an adult while practicing walking. ■ Provide small pieces of food for infants to practice their pincer grasp.

Source: Adapted from *Understanding Child Development* (7th ed.), by R. Charlesworth, 2007, Clifton Park, NY: Thomson Delmar Learning.

environment. Infant play is exploratory to start with, then becomes imitative and imaginative. Around 12 months—as memory increases and words emerge, infants begin engaging in pretend play. Play situations should usually include scaffolding from you, through playful interactions with infants. This process enhances brain development and the construction of concepts.

As you play with infants they will often look to you for cues on how to react to or evaluate a new situation. Your facial expressions, posture, voice tone, and language will provide information for infants to gauge their own behavior. You can also gauge their responses to your interaction from their cues. Individual infants will vary in their need for time alone and time spent interacting

TABLE 1—9   CHARACTERISTICS OF INFANT COGNITIVE DEVELOPMENT

Child's Name_____   Birth Date_____

Cognitive	Date
Birth to 1 month	
Blinks in response to fast-approaching object	
Follows a slowly moving object through a complete 180-degree arc	
Follows objects moved vertically if close to infant's face	
Continues looking about, even in the dark	
Begins to study own hand when lying in tonic-neck-reflex position	
Prefers to listen to mother's voice rather than a stranger's	
Frequently synchronizes body movements to speech patterns of caregiver	
Turns away from unpleasant odors	
1 to 4 months	
Fixes on a moving object held at 12 in. (30.5 cm)	
Continues to gaze in direction of moving objects that have disappeared but does not search for them	
Exhibits some sense of size/color/shape recognition of objects in the immediate environment	
Watches hands intently	
Alternates looking at an object, at one or both hands, and then back at the object	
Moves eyes from one object to another.	
Focuses on small object and reaches for it; usually follows own hand movements	
Attempts to keep toy in motion by moving arms and legs	
Begins to mouth objects	
4 to 8 months	
Turns in direction of sound and locates familiar voices and sounds	
Focuses on small objects and reaches for them	
Uses hand, mouth, and eyes in coordination to explore own body, toys, and surroundings	
Imitates actions, such as pat-a-cake, waving bye-bye, and playing peek-a-boo	
Shows fear of falling from high places, such as changing table, stairs	
Looks over side of crib or high chair for dropped objects; delights in repeatedly throwing objects overboard for adult to retrieve	
Drops one toy when handed another	
Will search for hidden object	
Plays actively with small objects	

(Continued)

TABLE 1−9 CHARACTERISTICS OF INFANT COGNITIVE DEVELOPMENT (*Continued*)

Cognitive	Date
4 to 8 months	
Bangs objects together playfully; bangs spoon or toy on table	
Enjoys playing in water at bath time	
8 to 12 months	
Watches people, objects, and activities in the immediate environment	
Shows awareness of distant objects (15 to 20 ft. away) by pointing at them	
Searches for a partially hidden object	
Puts everything in mouth	
Reaches for toys that are visible but out of reach	
Continues to drop first item when other toys or items are offered; may begin to drop toys intentionally	
Recognizes the reversal of an object—cup upside down is still a cup	
Shows appropriate use of everyday items: pretends to drink from a cup, hugs doll, etc.	
Imitates activities: hitting two blocks together, playing pat-a-cake, rolling a ball, etc.	
Follows simple directions	
Demonstrates functional relationships: puts spoon in mouth, turns pages to a book, etc.	
Spatial relationships—puts block in cup when requested	

Source: Adapted from *Developmental Profiles, Pre-Birth through Twelve* (5th ed.), by K. D. Allen & L. R. Marotz, 2007. Reprinted with permission of Delmar Learning, a division of Thomson Learning: http://www.thomsonrights.com. Fax 800 730-2215.

with others. Fussiness or distraction may indicate they need a change in stimulation. Following are some examples of interactions, activities, and materials to stimulate the cognitive development of infants:

- Play games such as peek-a-boo, pat-a-cake, and hide-and-seek. Adjust the rules by playing pat-a-cake using child's feet, or hide-and-seek by hiding a toy and leaving part of the toy visible.

- Engage in play by imitating infants' facial expressions (especially funny faces) and motor movements.

■ Encourage infants to participate in finger plays and songs by making sounds, mimicking movements (e.g., clapping), and using puppets or stuffed animals.

■ Make sensory bottles by collecting small bottles and filling them with beans, rice, or other objects that will make different sounds when shaken (make sure the lids can't be removed). Encourage the infants to shake them to hear different sounds.

■ During play and routines, describe objects, ask questions, and encourage exploration.

■ Have available a variety of the following types of materials:
  • Tactile discovery boxes, snap beads, balls, etc.
  • Large and small soft building blocks
  • Musical instrument shakers
  • Giant manipulative construction toys (links, star builders, Legos, etc.)
  • Shape sorters

LANGUAGE DEVELOPMENT

Infants enjoy and can participate in conversations long before they can speak (perhaps even before birth). By one month old infants can discriminate different languages and communicate needs for things such as sleep, feeding, or stimulation through cries. Three-month-olds begin to coo by making vowel sounds such as "oooh" and "aah." Around eight months, infants start to babble by repeating strings of consonant-vowel sounds such as "ma, ma, ma" or "da, da, da." By nine months, infant sounds start to resemble their native languages and they begin to use gestures that have meaning. At 10 months they begin to imitate words or sounds, and by one year most infants are using meaningful speech (*ba* = bye, *annna* = Amanda.) See Table 1–10.

Your Role: Supporting Language Development

There are several things you can do to ensure that the language abilities of all infants in your program get off to a great start. When you respond appropriately to infant cries and efforts of speech, it encourages infants to continue communicating their needs. Young infants tend to move their bodies in rhythm with adult speech, so talking to them or singing to them facilitates both motor and language development. Younger infants may also "talk to" objects,

TABLE 1–10 CHARACTERISTICS OF INFANT LANGUAGE DEVELOPMENT

Child's Name_____ Birth Date_____

Language	Date
Birth to 1 month	
Cries and fusses as major forms of communication	
Reacts to loud noises by blinking, moving (or stopping), shifting eyes, making a startle response	
Shows preference for certain sounds (music and human voices) by calming down or quieting	
Puts body movements in rhythm with speech patterns of adults	
Turns head to locate voices and other sounds	
Makes occasional sounds other than crying	
1 to 4 months	
Reacts to sounds (voice, rattle, doorbell); later will search for source by turning head	
Coordinates vocalizing, looking, and body movements in face-to-face exchanges with parent or caregiver	
Babbles or coos when spoken to or smiled at	
Will vocalize in rhythm with adult	
Imitates own sounds and single vowel sounds produced by others	
Laughs out loud	
4 to 8 months	
Responds appropriately to own name and simple requests, such as "eat," "wave bye-bye"	
Imitates some nonspeech sounds, such as cough, tongue click, lip smacking	
Produces a full range of vowels and some consonants: r, s, z, th, and w	
Responds to variations in the tone of voice of others	
Expresses emotions (pleasure, satisfaction, anger) by making different sounds	
"Talks" to toys	
Babbles by repeating same syllable in a series: (e.g., ba, ba, ba)	
8 to 12 months	
Babbles or jabbers to initiate social interaction; may shout to attract attention	
Shakes head for "no" and may nod for "yes"	
Responds by looking for voice when name is called	
Babbles in sentence-like sequences; followed by jargon (syllables/sounds with language-like inflection)	
Waves "bye-bye"; claps hands when asked	
Enjoys simple songs and rhymes	
Says "da-da" and "ma-ma"	

Source: Adapted from *Developmental Profiles, Pre-Birth through Twelve* (5th ed.), by K. D. Allen & L. R. Marotz, 2007, Clifton Park, NY: Thomson Delmar Learning. Reprinted with permission of Delmar Learning, a division of Thomson Learning: http://www.thomsonrights.com. Fax 800 730-2215.

while older infants start pointing at objects and people. Label things for them by pointing to the object and saying things like "You see the ball; it's a ball." You might repeat the label several times if the infant remains interested. Around nine months, infants begin using gestures and you can start teaching them simple sign language (e.g., put their hand to their mouth to indicate they want to drink or eat).

Infants also enjoy being read to from the time they are born. Reading to infants helps build cognitive and language abilities. Board books are recommended for infants and come in a wide variety, including books with pop-ups, tactile stimulation, and sounds. Many children's picture books are printed as board books. You should also use regular picture books to read to infants, and model appropriate care of books. For other activities that promote language development, see Table 1–11.

SOCIAL-EMOTIONAL DEVELOPMENT

Infants have complex, individual personalities and need social relationships. At birth infants display contentment and distress. Smiling and laughter develop during the next three months. By four to eight months, anger is expressed when efforts are frustrated. Near the end of the first year, fear, disgust, surprise, and humor have also emerged. During this time of rapid emotional growth, secure attachment to caregivers provides safety and security. Secure attachment grows from interactions that are sensitive and responsive. Young infants need consistent, dependable care that is responsive to their cues and needs. Social interactions with others from the time of birth teach infants how to identify, express, and regulate emotions. Communication patterns are based on reciprocity or exchanges of facial expressions, eye contact, gestures, and words and sounds between the infant and others. Infants must first learn to maintain their attention, then they use signals such as smiles, vocalizing, motor cues, and facial expressions to indicate that they want to interact (Charlesworth, 2008). See Table 1–12 on p. 41.

With practice, communication expands and infants try new types of interactions to test the reactions of others. By four to five months, infants initiate and lead social exchanges, deciding when to move their attention to other things by looking away. This helps them regulate stimulation and prevents them from becoming overwhelmed. Once infants gain the ability to move on their own,

TABLE 1–11   SUPPORTING INFANT LANGUAGE SKILLS SELF-CHECKLIST

	B	P	M
I converse with infants, especially during routine care such as diapering and feeding.			
I pause periodically during conversations with infants to allow them to participate either verbally or through movements.			
I encourage infants to imitate sounds.			
I acknowledge infant participation and continue conversations and vocalizations that express emotions.			
I make eye contact with infants while conversing with them.			
When infants turn their heads or look away, I stop interacting until they are ready to engage again.			
I carry infants around the room while describing people and things.			
I make class books with pictures of infants, parents, siblings, and teachers and laminate them for infants to use.			
I hold infants on my lap or position myself near them and hold the book at their eye level while reading to them.			
I point to the significant things in the illustrations while reading to infants and encourage them to point to and interact with books.			
I read at least one book with each infant individually each day.			
I provide infants with a wide variety of books, including books about animals, families, shapes, and colors.			
I sing songs and repeat nursery rhymes with infants.			

Directions: Use this checklist to evaluate your skills at communicating with infants.

Beginning (B): You are aware of and understand the criteria.

Progressing (P): You are implementing and experimenting with the criteria.

Mastery (M): You understand how to adapt the criteria to fit the individual needs of children.

Source: Adapted from *Make Way for Literacy*, G. Owocki, 2001. Portsmouth, NH: Heinemann.

caregivers become a secure base from which to explore. Infants frequently look back to caregivers for cues on how they should react to new situations. Between 9 and 14 months, separation anxiety begins (see Table 1–12). Reassurance and patience are vital elements of allowing infants time to adjust and become familiar with new events and people.

Temperament significantly influences the types of interactions individual infants prefer. Temperament characteristics include predictability of eating, sleeping, and elimination; the ability to adapt to

TABLE 1—12   CHARACTERISTICS OF INFANT SOCIAL-EMOTIONAL DEVELOPMENT

Child's Name_____   Birth Date_____

Social-Emotional Development	Date
Birth to 1 month	
Experiences a short period of alertness immediately following birth	
Likes to be held close and cuddled when awake	
Shows qualities of individuality in responding or not responding to similar situations	
Begins to establish emotional attachment or bonding with parents and caregivers	
Begins to develop a sense of security/trust with parents and caregivers; responses to different individuals vary	
1 to 4 months	
Imitates, maintains, terminates, and avoids interactions	
Reacts to familiar voices	
Reacts differently to variations in adult voices; frowns or looks anxious if voice is loud or unfamiliar	
Enjoys being held and cuddled at times other than feeding and bedtime	
Coos, gurgles, and squeals when awake	
Smiles in response to a friendly face or voice	
Entertains self for brief periods by playing with fingers, hands, and toes	
4 to 8 months	
Fully attached to mother or single caregiver; stranger anxiety beginning in later part of this stage	
Seeks attention with body movements or makes sounds	
Delights in observing surroundings; continuously watches people and activities	
Begins to develop an awareness of self as a separate individual from others	
Becomes more outgoing and social in nature—smiles, coos, reaches out	
Distinguishes among and responds differently to strangers, teachers, parents, siblings	
Responds differently and appropriately to facial expressions—frowns, smiles	
Imitates facial expressions, actions, and sounds	
8 to 12 months	
Exhibits a definite fear of strangers; clings to, or hides behind, parent or caregiver (stranger anxiety); resists separating from familiar adult (separation anxiety)	

(*Continued*)

TABLE 1–12   CHARACTERISTICS OF INFANT SOCIAL-EMOTIONAL DEVELOPMENT (*Continued*)

Social-Emotional Development	Date
8 to 12 months	
Enjoys being near and included in daily activities of family members and teachers; is becoming more sociable and outgoing	
Enjoys novel experiences and opportunities to examine new objects	
Shows need to be picked up and held by extending arms upward, crying, or clinging to adult's legs	
Offers toys and objects to others	
Begins to exhibit assertiveness by resisting caregiver's requests; may kick, scream, or throw self on the floor	

Source: Adapted from *Developmental Profiles, Pre-Birth through Twelve* (5th ed.), by K. D. Allen & L. R. Marotz, 2007, Clifton Park, NY: Thomson Delmar Learning. Reprinted with permission of Delmar Learning, a division of Thomson Learning: http://www.thomsonrights.com. Fax 800 730-2215.

new situations; sensitivity to sensory experiences; persistence; and how intensely emotions are felt and expressed (Thomas & Chess, 1977). Gillespie and Seibel (2006) point out that temperament characteristics are neither positive nor negative but should guide a caregiver's decisions concerning how to approach each infant. For instance, shy infants may need extra reassurance and encouragement to interact with peers, while infants with intense emotional responses need help developing calming strategies. Interactions that are sensitive, responsive, and tailored to the unique needs of each infant help infants grow into well-adjusted human beings.

Your Role: Supporting Social-Emotional Development

You have an important role in helping infants establish a sense of self and relationships with others. Providing sensitive, responsive interactions and care encourages language development, attachment, and emotional regulation. Engaging with infants in reciprocal interactions that are responsive to their individual temperaments sends the message that they are important and their efforts to communicate are heard. Focus on understanding and being responsive to the individual characteristics of infants. Playful interaction with adults and peers enhances infants' emotional development. Through play infants explore the world, themselves, and others.

At three months infants enjoy communicating with one another through gazing and movement. By six months infants may watch each other and vocalize sounds. At 6 to 12 months they communicate through touch, facial expressions, gestures, and imitating one another (Fogel, 2001). Your role is to facilitate interactions with peers and model appropriate social interaction. Use the Supporting Social-Emotional Development of Infants Self-Checklist (Table 1–13) to evaluate your practices, or ask a peer to observe your interactions and give you feedback.

DEVELOPMENTAL ALERTS

Infants with special needs may have genetic disorders, be premature, have birth defects, or develop sensory/motor difficulties as they grow. Early identification of such difficulties is critical. One of your roles is to watch for developmental difficulties so that treatment and support can begin as soon as possible. Early intervention programs, including mental health services, are available. These programs can help you and families meet the special needs of infants. Check with a health care provider or early childhood specialist if you notice sudden changes in behavior or if by one month of age, the infant

- does not show alarm or "startle" responses to loud noises.

- fails to suck and swallow with ease.

- does not show gains in height, weight, and head circumference.

- cannot grasp with equal strength with both hands.

- does not make eye-to-eye contact when awake and being held.

- does not become quiet soon after being picked up.

- does not roll head from side to side when placed on stomach.

- does not express needs and emotions with cries and patterns of vocalizations that can be distinguished from one another.

- does not stop crying when picked up and held.

By four months of age, the infant

- is not continuing to show steady increases in height, weight, and head circumference.

- does not smile in response to the smiles of others.

TABLE 1–13   SUPPORTING SOCIAL-EMOTIONAL DEVELOPMENT OF INFANTS SELF-CHECKLIST

	Rarely	Sometimes	Frequently
I help young infants increase their ability to maintain attention by gazing with them for longer periods of time.			
When infants look away, become irritable, or seem withdrawn, I respect their cues and stop interacting.			
I am responsive and read and react to infant cues during routines and play interactions. As they engage in and withdraw from interactions, I allow them to control their attention and regulate their emotions.			
I support infants and parents during separation by allowing infants to be left in smaller increments of time and helping parents feel comfortable by reassuring them and communicating in a variety of ways.			
I provide a secure base from which older infants can explore, by observing their activities, providing reassurance and encouragement verbally, through eye contact, facial expression, and tone of voice.			
I playfully engage infants in activities based on their individual preferences, temperament, and needs.			
I include infants in daily activities by conversing with them and describing actions and events.			
I encourage infants to interact with peers by placing younger infants where they can see peers, monitoring the interactions of older infants, and modeling appropriate interactions.			
I provide continuity and consistency by having only one or two adults interact with the same infant.			
I hold, touch, and carry infants frequently.			
I learn about the individual temperaments of infants through observations and parent interviews.			
I adapt my interactions, routines, and schedules to support the development of individual personality, preferences, and temperament.			
I learn about cultural differences in infant behaviors and adapt my interactions with infants to meet their needs for stimulation and social contact in a culturally and developmentally appropriate manner. (Watch parents for cues on how they interact with infants, but only adapt interactions if parent cues are appropriate.)			
Identify one goal for personal improvement and reevaluate your progress in two weeks. Goal:			

Source: Adapted from *Understanding Child Development* (7th ed.), by R. Charlesworth, 2008, Clifton Park, NY: Thomson Delmar Learning; and "Self-Regulation: A Cornerstone of Early Childhood Development," by L. G. Gillespie, & N. L. Seibel, 2006, *Young Children, 61*(4), 34–39.

- cannot follow a moving object with eyes focusing together.

- does not bring hands together over *midchest*.

- does not turn head to locate sounds.

- is not beginning to raise head and upper body when placed on stomach.

- does not reach for objects or familiar persons.

By eight months of age, the infant

- does not show even or steady gains in weight, height, and head circumference.

- does not explore own hands and objects placed in hands.

- does not hold and shake a rattle.

- is not smiling, babbling, and laughing out loud.

- does not search for hidden objects.

- does not use a pincer grasp to pick up food or objects.

- does not have an interest in playing games like "peek-a-boo."

- does not show interest in new or unusual sounds.

- does not reach for and grasp objects.

- cannot sit alone.

- is not beginning to eat "solid" (pureed) food.

By twelve months of age the infant

- does not blink when fast-moving objects approach the eyes.

- is not beginning to cut teeth.

- is not imitating simple sounds.

- does not follow simple verbal requests: *come, bye-bye*.

- cannot pull self to a standing position.

SUPPORTING FAMILIES OF INFANTS

Parents and family members must make major changes in their lives with the addition of an infant. You can help families adapt to these changes by showing empathy, modeling appropriate skills, and providing accurate parenting resources. Older infants begin to express separation anxiety. This can create feelings of guilt or concern for parents. Parents who are concerned will usually hesitate when their child begins to cry or stay longer when leaving their child. You can ease this process by allowing infants to be left at care gradually, building up to longer lengths of time, and helping parents feel welcome and comfortable. Quality child care that includes consistent supportive caregivers can enhance infant-parent attachment (Charlesworth, 2008) (see also "Supporting the Development of Toddlers" section). Most teachers find it helpful to collect information from families through questions (see Table 1–14). You might ask parents questions when conducting a home visit or in conversations when parents come and go each day, or create a questionnaire that parents can fill out and you can keep

TABLE 1–14   INFANT FAMILY QUESTIONNAIRE

Infant Family Questionnaire
Tell me about yourself and your family.
How have your life and the lives of your family members changed since the birth of your baby?
What types of support do you have in caring for your baby (pediatrician, family, friends, etc.)?
What has been the most surprising thing about your baby?
What do you enjoy most about being a parent?
What do you find frustrating about being a parent?
What things does your baby enjoy?
Is there anything about your baby you don't understand?
How has your baby adjusted to feeding and sleeping?
What is your baby's schedule?
Have you participated in any type of parent education, or would you like to?
What goals do you have for your baby?
Do you have any questions or concerns for me?

Source: Adapted from *Understanding Child Development* (7th ed.), by R. Charlesworth, 2008, Clifton Park, NY: Thomson Delmar Learning.

on file. Most parents enjoy sharing their concerns and information about their infants. However, too many questions at one time can feel overwhelming. Use good judgment, and follow the lead of parents.

RECOMMENDED READINGS

Hast, F., & Hollyfield, A. (2001). *Infant and toddler experiences.* Redleaf Press. (ISBN 1-929610-14-9). This book provides experiences involving curiosity, connection, and coordination. Simple descriptions are included with needed materials and recommendations.

Honig, A. S. (2002). *Secure relationships: Nurturing infant toddler attachment in early care settings.* National Association for the Education of Young Children. (ISBN 1-928896-03-0). This text covers key points of developing and building attachment with young children.

RECOMMENDED WEB SITES

American Academy of Pediatrics: http://www.aap.org. Provides information on development, health, and safety. Includes articles for parents on sleep, SIDS, shaken baby syndrome, crying, car seats, immunizations, nutrition and feeding, developmental milestones, illnesses, child abuse and neglect, and much more.

National Center on Birth Defects and Developmental Disabilities (NCBDDD): http://www.cdc.gov. Part of the Centers for Disease Control, the NCBDDD promotes the health of babies, children, and adults. The Web site contains information on public health issues in child development, child development milestones, and preventing developmental delays, as well as downloadable Positive Parenting Tips sheets available free of charge.

National Infant & Toddler Child Care Initiative: http://www. nccic.org. Provides information on infant and toddler initiatives for infants, toddlers, their families, and the child care providers that serve them in each state. Offers fact sheets about infants and toddlers nationwide. Explains how states are participating in infant and toddler initiatives.

National SIDS/Infant Death Resource Center: http://sidscenter.org. Provides information on SIDS in child care, such as providing a safe sleep environment and handling grief and loss, and includes a brochure about placing children on their backs for sleep and "tummy time" for play.

Zero to Three: http://www.zerotothree.org. The nation's leading resource on the first years of life. Provides publications, conferences, training, parent information from A–Z, articles, public policy information, a professional journal, brain research results, materials in Spanish, handouts, information on coping with trauma, and much more.

SUPPORTING THE DEVELOPMENT OF TODDLERS

Toddlers are curious and like to do things on their own. They enjoy discovering how the world works by experimenting with people and things. Each toddler is an individual with personal desires, preferences, experiences, and personality. This can lead to challenges as they assert and defend their sense of independence. However, well-planned toddler classrooms, led by thoughtful teachers, are exciting and filled with humor. This chapter provides some practical tips for creating a wonderful toddler classroom. It is organized by developmental domain—physical, motor, cognitive, language, and social-emotional development. At the end of this chapter developmental alerts are identified and some considerations for working with toddler families are provided. If you are working with toddlers it is recommended that you also review the sections covering infants and children aged three through six. This section begins with the physical growth of toddlers.

PHYSICAL GROWTH

During the second and third year physical growth slows, but steady gains in both height and weight are expected. More teeth emerge and dental care should become a regular health care routine (see Table 1–15). As brain growth continues, thinking becomes quicker. By 18 months, rapid brain development improves regulation of emotions and behavior, as well as attention span and memory. These abilities allow toddlers to take in sensory and emotional information, evaluate it, and decide how to act (BrainWonders, 1998–2001c). During this time, appropriate nutrition and health care are critical for continued physical growth and brain development.

TABLE 1—15   CHARACTERISTICS OF TODDLER PHYSICAL GROWTH

Child's Name_____   Birth Date _____

Physical	Date
One year	
Height increases 2–3 in. a year (avg. 32–35 in.)	
Weight avg. 21–27 lb, gains $1/_4$ to $1/_2$ lb per month (triples birth weight)	
Head circumference increases $1/_2$ in. per six months	
6 to 10 teeth erupt	
Vision 20/60	
Sleeps 10–12 hours night and naps; may have difficulty falling asleep ("winding down")	
Small appetite; at times will eat only a few preferred foods	
Two years	
Gains 2 to $2^1/_2$ lb per year; weighs 26–32 lb (about four times birth weight)	
Increases 3–5 in. in height per year; average height is 34–38 in.	
Second molars appear	
Develops strong likes and dislikes of foods, may be "picky"; generally eats well, but this fluctuates	

Source: Adapted from *Developmental Profiles, Pre-Birth through Twelve* (5th ed.), by K. D. Allen & L. R. Marotz, 2007, Clifton Park, NY: Thomson Delmar Learning. Reprinted with permission of Delmar Learning, a division of Thomson Learning: http://www.thomsonrights.com. Fax 800 730-2215.

Your Role: Supporting Physical Growth

Your role in supporting the healthy growth of toddlers includes preventing the spread of disease, providing a safe environment, and ensuring adequate nutrition. Daily, routine observations of toddlers can help you identify illness quickly. Toddlers remain vulnerable to respiratory viruses, colds, and other infections. They still explore through touch and mouthing objects, and they frequently put their hands in their mouths. Hand washing is one of the best measures to prevent illness. As toddlers increase in independence they can learn when and how to wash their hands, and usually will enjoy it (see Appendix A).

Toddlers are active and their growing abilities allow them access to various new situations (climbing; opening cupboards, drawers, doors, etc.). They need constant supervision. It is important to closely evaluate the environment. Discard any broken or unsafe items, cover outlets, use safety gates appropriately, make sure all cleaning supplies and medicines are secured and out of reach, identify and remove dangerous things they may try to climb on. A safe, healthy environment and sound nutrition will provide a sure foundation for future development.

Nutrition

Nutrition is a critical element for growing toddlers. Toddlers have small stomachs and use a lot of calories. Your role is to provide adequate nutrition by offering frequent, small, nutritious meals and snacks. It is not unusual for toddlers to fluctuate in their appetite and food preferences. At times it may seem as if they are hardly eating at all, and food preferences may change daily. Often this is part of their efforts to self-regulate and gain independence. Continue to offer healthy food choices and monitor gains in weight and height. Consult a health care provider if a toddler is not gaining steadily. When formula or breast milk is stopped, toddlers should receive whole milk products that provide the essential fats necessary for myelination in the brain. Other considerations include (BrainWonders, 1998–2001b):

- Avoid serving sweets and junk food in the classroom. Offer water and milk rather than sweetened drinks (juice, soda, or punch).

- Provide foods they can eat by themselves. This is also good practice for developing fine motor skills and hand-eye coordination. Encourage their attempts to self-feed. When spills occur, encourage their help in cleaning things up.

- Keep meal times pleasant and avoid conflicts over food. Most children will eat what they need if they are hungry and are offered small, frequent meals throughout the day.

- Be sensitive that different families and cultures have various eating behaviors and food preferences. Respect these differences and integrate them with classroom practices, when appropriate.

- Avoid using food as a reward or punishment. This will help toddlers develop a healthy attitude toward food.

- Have toddlers help prepare food. They are more likely to eat things they have helped prepare. They can also help set the table and pour drinks from small containers.

MOTOR DEVELOPMENT

The toddler years begin with movement as the central focus. Refining motor abilities allow children to do more for themselves, leading to cognitive, social, emotional, and language growth. Toddlers love to repeat things again and again. Through this process they proudly master skills and build coordination. By the second year, movements become smoother examples of this include the ability to run and use utensils to eat (see Table 1–16). Growing motor skills give toddlers a sense of pride as they actively pursue and accomplish the things they desire. However, their judgment skills are lacking and thus they tend to be impulsive. Learning self-regulation of motor skills helps promote healthy development. Toddlers need to learn what is acceptable while having opportunities to explore.

Your Role: Supporting Motor Development

Toddlers are active and fun-loving. Your role in supporting their motor development is to provide an appropriate environment where they can practice developing skills and gain confidence in self-regulation. Observe motor skills carefully and plan activities that are challenging but achievable, using appropriate materials, so that toddlers feel successful with their growing abilities. Give toddlers time to practice skills, space to explore, and encouragement. Independence can be facilitated by arranging the environment so that toddlers can do as much for themselves as possible. Toileting is one of the things toddlers will begin to do for themselves, and your role will be to assist families in the process of the toileting their toddlers. Next, a few suggestions on arranging the environment, selecting materials, and toileting are provided.

Environment

The saying "An ounce of prevention is worth a pound of cure" is very applicable in a toddler classroom. An appropriately arranged physical environment will prevent many mishaps and conflicts. Keep in mind that toddlers are curious and want to explore everything. They need a wide variety of novel and interesting things to explore. Their coordination is developing and they need sturdy toys that can be dropped and banged. They enjoy cause-and-effect toys, and things that allow them to repeat behaviors (e.g., pounding). They may still put things in their mouths, and thus need toys larger than $1^{1}/_{2}$ to 2 inches in diameter to avoid choking hazards.

TABLE 1—16 CHARACTERISTICS OF TODDLER MOTOR DEVELOPMENT

Child's Name_____   Birth Date _____

Motor Development	Date
One year	
Gross motor	
Crawls skillfully and quickly; gets to feet unaided	
Crawls up and down stairs	
Stands alone with feet spread apart, legs stiffened, and arms extended for support	
Walks unassisted near the end of this period (most children); falls often; not always able to maneuver around furniture or toys	
Uses furniture to lower self to floor; collapses backward into a sitting position or falls forward on hands and then sits	
Sits in a small chair	
Fine motor	
Releases an object voluntarily	
Picks up objects and throws them	
Carries toys from place to place	
Enjoys pushing or pulling toys while walking	
Holds crayon and uses whole arm movement to scribble	
Can help turn pages in a book	
Stacks two to four objects	
Pounds wooden pegs with a toy hammer	
Self-help	
Helps feed self; holds spoon; drinks from cup	
Often misses mouth, spills frequently	
May still eat with fingers	
Two years	
Gross motor	
Walks with a more erect, heel-to-toe pattern; can maneuver around obstacles in pathway	
Runs with greater confidence; has fewer falls	
Squats for long periods while playing	
Climbs stairs unassisted (but not with alternating feet)	
Uses feet to propel wheeled toy	

(Continued)

TABLE 1–16 CHARACTERISTICS OF TODDLER MOTOR DEVELOPMENT (*Continued*)	
Climbs on chair, turns around, sits down	
Throws large ball underhand without falling	
Balances on one foot (for a few moments); jumps up and down, but may fall	
Fine motor	
Fits large pegs in pegboard	
Turns knob to open door	
Uses fist to grasp crayon and scribble on large paper	
Likes to pour and fill (sand, water, etc.)	
Stacks four to six objects	
Puts objects together and takes them apart	
Self-help	
Holds cup in one hand, spills frequently	
Unbuttons large buttons	
Unzips large zippers	
Can feed self with increasing skill	
Tries to wash self in the bath	
Tries to dress self	
Can usually remove clothing	
Stays dry longer; may be willing to sit on toilet for a few minutes	
Begins to achieve toilet training during the second year (depending on physical and neurological development), although accidents should still be expected; will indicate readiness for toilet training	

Source: Adapted from *Developmental Profiles, Pre-Birth through twelve* (5th ed.), by K. D. Allen & L. R. Marotz, 2007, Clifton Park, NY: Thomson Delmar Learning. Reprinted with permission of Delmar Learning, a division of Thomson Learning: http://www.thomsonrights.com. Fax 800 730-2215.

Toddlers feel independent when they can move things by carrying baskets or pushing wagons. Check the effectiveness of your curriculum in promoting toddler motor and self-help skills with the checklist in Table 1–17. Here are some suggestions for arranging a classroom for toddlers.

- Set up the room with spaces for two to four toddlers to play together.

- Make sure there is a plentiful amount of toys that toddlers can choose from on their own. Provide duplicates to prevent conflicts and encourage imitation.

TABLE 1—17　MATERIALS AND ACTIVITIES FOR MOTOR DEVELOPMENT SELF-CHECKLIST

	Rarely	Sometimes	Frequently
1. Movement games that provide anticipation are played (e.g., "hide-and-seek," "duck, duck, goose," etc.).			
2. Cause-and-effect movement games are played (e.g., "ring around the roses," "London bridge").			
3. Toys are available that allow children to experiment with cause and effect (balls that roll down some type of slide, lock boxes with doors to open and close, toys with levers to pull or buttons to push, etc.).			
4. Open-ended and sensory materials such as play dough, sand, water, blocks, paint, and art material are available. Accessories such as clay-working tools, paintbrushes, and spring-action scissors for squeezing are provided.			
5. Tunnels toddlers can crawl through and ramps to slide on are provided.			
6. Toys that encourage climbing, running, riding, and jumping are plentiful.			
7. Giant pegboards, stacking toys, sensory bottles or tubes, construction toys that link together, stringing beads, simple puzzles, dressing boards, and pounding toys are provided to facilitate fine motor and self-help skills.			
8. Toys that require gross motor skills, including pushing and pulling or containers to carry and dump things (purses, baskets), are provided.			
9. Toys for imitating and imaginative play—such as vacuum, shopping carts, lawn mowers, wagons, strollers, people figures, animal figures, small cars and trucks, dolls, plastic dishes and food, hats, dress-up clothes, telephones, scarves, fabrics, and literacy materials (magazines, shopping lists, etc.)—are provided.			

Identify one goal for personal improvement and reevaluate your progress in two weeks.

Goal:

Source: Adapted from "Using Everyday Materials to Promote Problem Solving in Toddlers," by L. Segatti, J. Brown-DuPaul, & T. L. Keyes, 2003, *Young Children, 58*(5), 12–16.

- Provide space for chasing, jumping, and running, as well as plenty of outdoor time.

- Provide gross motor activities to improve social cooperation, as well as opportunities for imaginative play. Examples include: sensory balls, cooperative riding toys, bridges, ladders, wagons, and large hollow blocks.

- Toddlers love to climb. Consider having a small indoor climber with safety mats underneath. This may prevent their attempts to climb on shelves, tables, and other inappropriate places.

- Plan activities using music and movement to teach concepts of spatial awareness and control of movements. Use scarves or ribbons to enhance movement.

- Choose furnishings that are child sized, and provide step stools so that children can be independent when toileting or washing hands.

- Display materials on low shelves and organize them so that toddlers can access things themselves.

Toileting

Toddler mastery of toileting is a milestone most parents look forward to. Helping families of toddlers with the process of toileting requires identifying readiness and negotiating appropriate methods with parents. Parents may have specific ideas about toileting that you don't feel are appropriate. This is usually due to differences in personality, cultural background, and knowledge of child development.

Bainer and Hale (2000) point out that it is important for teachers to remember that parents are still learning parenting skills. You can best support parents by providing information and discussing options in order to agree upon a method that will be consistent for children. Clear communication and relaxed, consistent practices between home and school will help ease this process for toddlers. Signs of readiness include (Bainer & Hale, 2000; Riblatt, Obegi, Hammons, Ganger, & Ganger, 2003):

- emotional readiness (avoid beginning toileting at stressful time, such as the birth of a sibling, move, divorce, death in the family, etc.).

- interest in using the toilet.

- interest in underwear.

- being aware of elimination.

- ability to communicate the need to eliminate.

When parents and toddlers are ready to begin toileting, Bainer and Hale (2000) and Ritblatt et al. (2003) have the following suggestions for caregivers.

- Recognize that the toddler is in charge of this process—you are there to support them.

- Be perceptive of individual children's cues and listen to them.

- Encourage toddlers to be as independent as possible. Use step stools and clip-on toilet rings to make the toilet safe and accessible. Encourage clothing the child can remove and replace as independently as possible.

- Play toileting using doll house figures, dramatic play props, and puppets.

- Read books about toileting.

- Plan for and expect accidents. Have parents bring several pairs of extra clothes.

- Handle accidents in a matter-of-fact way. Bathe and change the toddler if needed, then take the toddler to the toilet or potty chair and discuss how the body feels when needing to go potty. Encourage the child to participate in cleaning up accidents as much as possible. Make sure that what you say and do communicates to children that you trust them and know they will succeed as they keep trying.

- Be patient and provide encouragement to both parents and children.

- Avoid any practices that would lead to feelings of shame or guilt.

Family culture and special needs will impact when and how toileting occur. Respect for individual needs and values, patience, and clear communication will help you navigate this process with parents. Specific questions to ask parents about toileting include:

- Do you feel relaxed about toileting or pressured to get it done?

- Has anyone given you advice about toilet training, or have you read any information? If so, what? What did you think about it?

- Have you ever put your toddler on the toilet? When? Why? What happened?

- When do you think is a good time to start toilet training?

- Does your toddler show any interest in the toilet? If so, what?

- What procedures (including language) would you like to use in toilet training?

COGNITIVE DEVELOPMENT

The characteristics of curiosity and independence result in toddlers who enjoy repeating actions and experimenting. Toddlers explore through touch, taste, sight, and smell as they continually seek to solve problems. Through play and imitation toddlers build concepts such as size, shape, number, and classification. They are able to classify or categorize things with similar characteristics into groups, but still tend to notice the most obvious characteristic (e.g., *all animals are dogs*). As symbolic thought develops, cognitive skills and language skills enhance each other. Problem-solving skills evolve as toddlers from 12 to 18 months develop increased memory capabilities. They can remember a behavior they see and repeat it later. At about 18 months, toddlers reach the final stage of *object permanence* (remembering that an object exists even if they cannot see it) and begin to think through problems before acting (see Table 1–18). Between 18 and 24 months, language expands, as well as the ability to pretend. At about 24 to 36 months, play through language and movement helps toddlers develop problem-solving skills, as the brain continues to build and refine connections (BrainWonders, 1998–2001c; Piaget & Inhelder, 1969).

Your Role: Supporting Cognitive Development

Toddlers need to manipulate objects, problem solve, imitate, and explore concepts such as size, shape, number, and classification. Meaningful curriculum for toddlers is based on their interests. For example, toddlers who notice bugs on the playground may be ready to investigate concepts related to living things. Your role is to observe and listen to the interests of toddlers. Toddlers may wonder about things that adults take for granted, such as "Where does the

TABLE 1—18   CHARACTERISTICS OF TODDLER COGNITIVE DEVELOPMENT

Child's Name_____   Birth Date _____

Cognitive Development	Date
1 year	
Enjoys object-hiding activities: early on, will search same location for a hidden object; later will search in several locations	
Passes toy to other hand when offered a second object ("crossing the midline")	
Manages three to four objects by setting an object aside (on lap or floor) when presented with a new toy	
Puts toys in mouth less often	
Demonstrates understanding of functional relationships (objects that belong together)	
Starts to discriminate space and form; places objects in simple puzzle	
Puts objects in container and dumps them out	
Names everyday objects	
2 years	
Exhibits better-coordinated eye-hand movements; can put objects together, take them apart; fits large pegs into pegboard	
Begins to use objects for purposes other than intended (pushes block around as a boat)	
Completes classification based on one dimension (separates toy dinosaurs from toy cars)	
Stares for long moments; seems fascinated by, or engrossed in, figuring out a situation	
Attends to self-selected activities for longer periods of time	
Looks for hidden object in the last hiding place first	
Shows discovery of cause and effect: squeezing the cat makes her scratch	

Source: Adapted from *Developmental Profiles, Pre-Birth through Twelve* (5th ed.), by K. D. Allen & L. R. Marotz, 2007, Clifton Park, NY: Thomson Delmar Learning. Reprinted with permission of Delmar Learning, a division of Thomson Learning: http://www.thomsonrights.com. Fax 800 730-2215.

water go when the toilet is flushed?" Once you have identified the interest of toddlers your role is to guide toddlers through solving problems that are of interest to them. Da Ros and Kovach (1998) suggest waiting to help toddlers to give them opportunities to solve problems themselves when appropriate, and intervening to explain a situation and prevent harm. As you interact with toddlers, allow them time to problem solve on their own, and watch carefully for cues that indicate they are unable to find a solution before intervening. When offering help, first try asking them a question to help clarify the problem or options, after which you may have to make a suggestion.

Segatti, Brown-DuPaul, and Keyes (2003) found that providing open-ended experiences with opportunities to make decisions is an important aspect of spontaneous problem solving. Materials that can be used in a variety of ways to elicit the curiosity of children are wise choices. Some examples include the following (Charlesworth, 2008; Herr & Swim, 1998; Segatti et al. 2003):

- Encourage pretend play by providing a variety of dress-up clothes and accessories: silly things; dress-ups with large buttons, zippers, or snaps; everyday household items to encourage role play, imitation, and symbolic thought (boxes, paper chip canisters, scarves, alarm clock, etc.).

- Play language games by changing the words in common songs and rhymes that children are familiar with (they especially enjoy it if you include their name).

- Play variations of hide-and-seek games (toddlers may need to watch the toy being hidden).

- Model pretend play by extending what they are doing with pretend sounds or pretend actions, such as pretending to eat. Avoid directing play; follow their lead.

- Engage in conversations about things toddlers are doing. Ask them open-ended questions such as "What would happen if . . .?"

- Play classification games by providing a variety of objects that can be sorted and asking toddlers to make collections of things that are, for example, green, round, or have fur, and talking to them about similarities and differences (pom-poms, metal lids, large plastic rings, etc.).

- Help them make books about classroom happenings, their families, and concepts they are learning, for them to review and enjoy.

LANGUAGE DEVELOPMENT

During the toddler years, language expands by leaps and bounds. This begins when toddlers utter their first attempts at meaningful speech (about 12 months). These first words are sometimes unclear but usually refer to important objects or people (maybe even you). Words become clearer but are still approximations. Some sounds may be substituted or left out (e.g., "bak" means "duck"). Next, toddlers begin to use one word to convey an entire thought—"up" means "pick me up" (holophrase). During the second year they may lose interest in toys and desire to be near adults, focusing on speech. Don't be surprised if they demand verbal interaction with you, want you to label objects, and watch your mouth as you talk (Cawfield, 1992). Near the second year toddlers begin using "telegraphic" speech, which consists of two- to three-word sentences (e.g., "want milk") (see Table 1–19). While observing this process keep in mind that toddlers can understand more than they can speak. This may increase feelings of frustration if they are not understood, and it is important to ask them to point to things and observe nonverbal cues (Charlesworth, 2008).

Your Role: Supporting Language Development

The best ways to support the emerging language skills of toddlers is to engage in conversations with them and model literacy skills. Use a wide variety of words when conversing with them. Talk with them by explaining expectations, labeling things, asking questions about their families, talking about feelings, and helping them solve problems, and encourage them to converse with one another. When a toddler's first language differs from English, encourage the first language, while exposing the toddler to English in a relaxed way (see "Special Needs" section for ideas in this chapter).

Toddlers can also learn basic literacy concepts such as reading is fun, how to treat books, and that print has meaning (McGee & Richgel, 2004). Provide a variety of books for toddlers. When reading to toddlers, remember that they have a short attention span. Read to toddlers in small groups to provide more opportunities for them to ask questions, point at and label things in pictures, and share ideas. Plan time in your schedule for reading books; try reading during meals and transitions. The checklist in Table 1–20 (see p. 63) has additional practices. Recommended readings for toddlers appear in Table 1–21 (see p. 64).

TABLE 1—19   CHARACTERISTICS OF TODDLER LANGUAGE DEVELOPMENTT

Child's Name_____   Date _____

Language Development	Date
1 year	
Produces considerable "jargon": combines words/sounds into speech-like patterns	
Shows understanding of conversational exchange	
Joins in and enjoys songs and rhymes	
Uses one word to convey an entire thought (holophrastic speech); later, produces two-word phrases to express a complete thought (telegraphic speech)	
Follows simple directions: "Give Daddy the cup"	
Points to familiar persons, animals, and toys when asked	
Identifies three body parts if someone names them: "Show me your nose (toe, ear)"	
Uses gestures to direct adult attention	
Uses 5 to 50 words	
25–50 percent of speech is understandable	
Responds to simple questions with "yes" or "no" and appropriate head movement.	
Indicates a few desired objects/activities by name: "bye-bye," "cookie"; verbal request is often accompanied by an insistent gesture	
2 years	
Enjoys being read to if allowed to point, make relevant noises, turn pages	
Realizes that language is effective for getting others to respond to needs and preferences	
Uses 50 to 300 different words; vocabulary continuously increasing	
Has broken linguistic code; in other words, much of a two-year-old's talk has meaning to him or her	
Understands more language than can communicate verbally; most two-year-olds' receptive language is more developed than their expressive language	
Negates statements by adding "no" (e.g., "no milk")	
Talks about objects or people not in the immediate environment	
65–75 percent of speech is understandable	
May stammer or use substitute sounds	
Uses some plurals	
Frequently asks "what's that?"	
Utters three- and four-word statements; uses conventional word order to form more complete sentences (telegraphic speech)	

Source: Adapted from *Developmental Profiles, Pre-Birth through Twelve* (5th ed.), by K. D. Allen & L. R. Marotz, 2007, Clifton Park, NY: Thomson Delmar Learning. Reprinted with permission of Delmar Learning, a division of Thomson Learning: http://www.thomsonrights.com. Fax 800 730-2215.

TABLE 1—20   SUPPORTING TODDLER LANGUAGE SKILLS SELF-CHECKLIST

	Rarely	Sometimes	Frequently
1. I repeat songs and stories toddlers enjoy.			
2. I name objects while facing toddlers so they can see the movements of my mouth.			
3. I show toddlers that their ideas are important and that print has meaning by writing down things toddlers say and do.			
4. I elaborate stories, songs, and nursery rhymes by using simple props such as puppets or hats.			
5. Toddlers are taught to treat books with care.			
6. I model appropriate use and care of books.			
7. I point to words while I'm reading.			
8. I make meaningful books with toddlers about families, classroom happenings, peers, and everyday events.			
9. I encourage toddlers to point to pictures and talk about them.			
10. I talk with toddlers about the story, ask them questions, and extend what they say.			
11. I encourage toddlers to make comments about activities and books.			
12. I spend individual time reading to toddlers, sit near them, or hold them on my lap with the book at their eye level.			
Identify one goal for personal improvement and reevaluate in two weeks.			
Goal:			

Source: Adapted from *Make Way for Literacy,* by G. Owocki, 2001, Portsmouth, NH: Heinemann.

SOCIAL-EMOTIONAL DEVELOPMENT

Play provides toddlers with opportunities to practice things and experiment with roles. Self-concept is developed as toddlers actively choose people to imitate and activities to engage in. In this context they can safely experiment with how their actions affect others (Bergan, 2001). Play with peers begins as toddlers play side by side with one another (see Table 1–22 on p. 65). With practice they engage with one another, and through play they develop social skills such as sharing of toys and not hitting. Toddlers also imitate, exchange toys, and have conflicts with each other. They do best when playing with peers in pairs or small groups. Near the beginning of the third year they seek approval from adults and experience feelings of success and failure. Keep in mind that toddlers are

TABLE 1–21   SUGGESTED AUTHORS AND BOOKS FOR TODDLERS
Eric Carle
The Very Hungry Caterpillar
Have You Seen My Cat?
Donald Crews
Freight Train
Harbor
Truck
School Bus
Flying
Sue Williams and Julie Vivas
I Went Walking
Bill Martin Jr. and Eric Carle
Brown Bear, Brown Bear, What Do You See?
Polar Bear, Polar Bear, What Do You Hear?
Sam McBratney
Guess How Much I Love You?
Margaret Wise Brown and Clement Hurd
Good Night Moon
Audrey Wood
Silly Sally

still learning how to apply behaviors to new situations and need practice in many situations to master rules. Patient, positive responses and accurate feedback send the message to toddlers that they are accepted and will succeed (Charlesworth, 2008).

Your Role: Supporting Social-Emotional Development

This can be a challenging and busy time for teachers. Toddlers need to develop cooperative prosocial behaviors, including the ability to have relationships with other children and adults, the ability to negotiate conflicts, a positive sense of self, and decision-making skills. Safe, nurturing home and school environments are critical for the development of these skills.

Toddlers are watching everyone carefully and experimenting with behaviors. Some toddlers may be learning one culture at

TABLE 1–22 CHARACTERISTICS OF SOCIAL-EMOTIONAL TODDLER DEVELOPMENT

Child's Name_____   Birth Date _____

Social-Emotional Development	Date
1 year	
Remains friendly toward others; usually less wary of strangers	
Helps pick up and put away toys	
Plays alone for short periods and does not play cooperatively	
Enjoys being held and read to	
Imitates adult actions in play	
Recognizes self in the mirror	
Enjoys other children/parallel play	
May have tantrum when tired or frustrated	
Very curious—may get into trouble if not supervised	
Asserts independence; wants to dress, bathe, eat without help	
Enjoys adult attention; likes to know that an adult is near; gives hugs and kisses	
2 years	
Shows empathy and caring	
Continues to use physical aggression if frustrated or angry (more exaggerated in some children); physical aggression lessens as verbal skills improve	
Expresses frustration through temper tantrums; tantrum frequency peaks during this year; cannot be reasoned with while tantrum is in progress	
Finds it difficult to wait or take turns; often impatient	
Enjoys "helping" with household chores; imitates everyday activities	
Usually plays alone but observes and may imitate older children	
Possessive of toys, but may occasionally offer a toy to another child.	
Defiant—shouts "no"	
Wants routines to stay the same	
Difficulty making choices—wants it both ways	
Orders parents and teachers around; makes demands and expects immediate compliance	

Source: Adapted from *Developmental Profiles, Pre-Birth through Twelve* (5th ed.), by K. D. Allen & L. R. Marotz, 2007, Clifton Park, NY: Thomson Delmar Learning. Reprinted with permission of Delmar Learning, a division of Thomson Learning: http://www.thomsonrights.com. Fax 800 730-2215.

home and another at school. It is important to learn about the culture of each toddler in your class. Be aware of your own behavior and avoid treating children in stereotypical (gender or cultural) ways. This will help you build relationships with families, develop empathy in children, and provide continuity between home and school (Quann & Wien, 2006). The following information provides suggestions for supporting the development of social skills and providing appropriate guidance.

Social Skills

Secure feelings of attachment to you will help toddlers interact more positively with peers. Take time to establish deep, caring relationships with each toddler. A behavior as simple as smiling communicates that you enjoy your relationship with them. Da Ros and Kovach (1998) suggest that when conflicts occur, most adults jump in too soon and solve the problem before the toddlers have an opportunity to negotiate. They recommend allowing toddlers opportunities to make autonomous decisions and problem solve. If no one is in danger of physical harm, try the following:

- Observe close by while toddlers negotiate.

- When they need help, explain the situation and offer nonevaluative suggestions such as "Maybe you could tell him you want the car."

- Avoid having toddlers make restitution that is not meaningful (e.g., making them say "I'm sorry"). Instead focus on what they can do to help (e.g., give the toy back).

Sometimes toddlers need help making contact with other toddlers; watch their play for signs that they need help negotiating, then explain the behaviors of other children to them and offer suggestions for initiating contact. Other ideas include (Charlesworth, 2008):

- When engaging in pretend play with toddlers, extend their ideas to include prosocial skills, such as caring for babies and sharing with others.

- Encourage helping behaviors such as comforting a hurt peer and sharing and respecting feelings.

- Acknowledge, accept, define, and talk about emotions.

- Purposefully teach and model prosocial behaviors using books, role-play, conversations, and everyday classroom situations.

Guidance

As self-concept emerges, toddlers become aware that you and other adults think about things differently than they do. Toddlers may begin testing your reactions in order to better understand what you are thinking and what is appropriate (Charlesworth, 2008). Your role is to provide guidance to help toddlers balance their need for autonomy and independence with self-regulation. It's important that children understand when behavior is inappropriate. Guiding toddlers means setting—and teaching—clear, simple limits that protect toddlers from physical and emotional harm. This includes avoiding any forms of discipline that would shame or humiliate. Toddlers can be surprisingly cooperative or extremely defiant as they learn to manage their growing independence. Guidance strategies to try with toddlers include the following:

- Be proactive; that is, foresee possible problems and prevent them from happening. An example of this is rearranging the environment so that toddlers have more small areas to work in rather than functioning in larger groups. Or, if you notice the toddlers in your class becoming restless, you might make an adjustment in your schedule to go outside earlier (Da Ros & Kovach, 1998).

- Use a combination of verbal and nonverbal actions to give toddlers positive feedback for appropriate behavior (Charlesworth, 2008).

- Substitute an incompatible appropriate behavior for an inappropriate behavior. For example, with a toddler who likes to play in the toilet, each time the toddler opens the lid, the adult says "shut it" while helping the toddler close the lid (Charlesworth, 2008).

- Redirect the toddler's behavior to more appropriate behavior. For example, if the toddler is running around the room, lead the child to the music center and choose a movement song to follow (Charlesworth, 2008).

- Provide opportunities for toddlers to function by themselves whenever possible (small step stools by sinks, low cubbies, etc.) and offer them choices whenever possible.

- Set simple, clear expectations that tell them what the expected behavior is. For example, "Keep your feet on the floor" rather than "Don't stand on the chair." Be firm yet kind.

- Consistently enforce consequences. Toddlers need to trust that expectations are firm and choices have consequences.

- Be patient and give reminders. Toddlers have difficulty transferring learning from one situation to another. They need many experiences before they can apply guidelines for behavior across situations.

- Acknowledge and identify their feelings (e.g., "You're angry that you have to come inside now.") and teach toddlers appropriate ways to express feelings.

- Watch their facial expressions. Notice when they are working to control anger and frustration, then support them with encouraging words or a reassuring touch.

- Shadow or stay close to toddlers learning to control aggressive urges, such as biting or hitting. Identify what happens before the behavior. Intervene before the toddler hits or bites by putting your hand on her or putting your arm around her shoulder. Then model appropriate vocabulary and actions for the situation. Encourage attempts at self-control.

- Support them in developing autonomy by encouraging participation in real work activities (e.g., sweeping floors, wiping tables, etc.). Help them participate by simplifying tasks and instructions to their level. Through this process you help them with things they desire to do, but are too difficult for them to accomplish on their own.

DEVELOPMENTAL ALERTS

Toddlers with special needs may have genetic disorders, developmental delays, sensory/motor difficulties, or speech and language disorders. Early identification of such difficulties is essential for optimal treatment. Early intervention programs can help you and families meet the special needs of toddlers (see Special Needs Section). Check with a health care provider or early childhood specialist if you notice sudden changes in behavior or if by 24 months of age, the toddler

- is not attempting to talk or repeat words.

- does not understand some new words.

- can not respond to simple questions with "yes" or "no."

- does not walk alone (or with very little help).

- rarely exhibit a variety of emotions: anger, delight, fear.

- is not interested in pictures.

- cannot recognize self in mirror.

- does not attempt self-feeding, like holding own cup to mouth and drinking.

If by the third birthday, the child

- is not eating a fairly well-rounded diet, even though amounts are small.

- cannot walk confidently with few stumbles or falls; climb steps with help.

- cannot avoid bumping into objects.

- does not carry out simple, two-step directions: "Come to Daddy and bring your book"; express desires, and ask questions.

- is not pointing to and naming familiar objects; using two- or three-word sentences.

- does not enjoy being read to.

- does not show interest in playing with other children: watching, perhaps imitating.

- is not beginning to show an interest in toilet training.

- cannot sort familiar objects according to a single characteristic, such as type, color, or size.

Adapted from *Developmental Profiles, Pre-Birth Through Twelve* (5th ed.), by K. D. Allen & L. R. Marotz, 2007. Reprinted with permission of Delmar Learning, a division of Thomson Learning: http://www.thomsonrights. com. Fax 800 730-2215.

SUPPORTING FAMILIES OF TODDLERS

To help toddlers learn self-control, cope with separation anxiety, and master toileting, you will need to work closely with families. Strong partnerships with families help provide consistent routines and expectations for the developing toddler. Families will differ in their expectations, discipline styles, communication styles, value of autonomy, and cooperation level. It can be challenging to find a fit between teaching and parenting styles. Communication and education are pertinent to navigating this process (see also "Supporting Diverse Families" section).

One of the most important opportunities you have to support families with toddlers is when a parent leaves the toddler in your classroom for the day. As toddlers gain increasing abilities to express their emotions, their reaction to separation usually increases. This is a surprise for many parents whose infants and young toddlers have been separating without difficulty. Parents may fear that their toddler is having difficulty at school or that they are doing something wrong. Parents need reassurance that this is expected, and that most toddlers work through this issue during the second year.

Balaban (2006) points out that it is also important for parents and caregivers to see things from the child's point of view. Children's feelings of anxiety come from not understanding what will happen next, and although they seek to be more independent they still feel vulnerable and scared at times. How parents and caregivers react sends a powerful message to children about their anxiety and their feelings of attachment. Parents and caregivers should expect some regression in other behaviors while children are working through separation anxiety. Children may also continue to feel anxious and miss parents even if they are not displaying separation anxiety. Balaban suggests some of the following strategies for helping toddlers and parents work through the separation process.

- Offer an individual introduction to the classroom. Set up a time (outside of regular class hours) when new toddlers can come see the classroom and meet you.

- Make plans with parents beforehand. Ask parents if they have talked with their toddler about saying "good-bye." Do they have a routine? How does their toddler usually react? What things help their toddler adjust? Do the parents have any concerns about leaving their toddler? Partner with parents to provide a transition object that reminds children of parents (e.g., blanket, toy, picture, etc.).

- Encourage parents to avoid leaving when their toddler is tired, hungry, or sick.

- Encourage parents to give a simple explanation to the toddler of why they need to leave, reassure the toddler they will be back, and develop a consistent but short good-bye routine. It may be good for parents to stay and play for a few minutes, but avoid making leaving a "big deal."

- Often, parents who leave a crying toddler visualize their toddler crying until they return. This increases the anxiety and guilt parents feel. Reassure parents that you will call them when their toddler calms down, or take a picture of the child playing happily and give it to parents at the end of the day.

- Try comforting crying toddlers by using puppets, people figures, or dolls to role-play parents leaving, going to work, and coming back.

- Help toddlers write a note to their parents. You may have to help them interpret their feelings due to limited language abilities. For instance, you might write the following letter with them: "Dear Mom, I didn't want you to go. I want you to stay with me. I miss you." Later that day you might help the toddler add: "I am playing blocks with Maria. We like knocking down towers. I'll be glad to see you soon." Have the toddler share the note with parents at the end of the day. Be sure parents know this is a coping strategy and not a guilt tactic.

TABLE 1–23   TODDLER FAMILY QUESTIONNAIRE
Toddler Family Questionnaire
What are your toddler's favorite play activities?
Do you feel your toddler is beginning to understand right and wrong? How can you tell?
Does your toddler have difficulty when you leave?
Do you have a "good-bye" routine? If so, please explain.
How do you feel about leaving your toddler in child care?
What helps to calm your toddler down?
What is your toddler's schedule?
Does your toddler have any behaviors that concern you?
What discipline techniques do you use?
Does your toddler view media? If yes, what types and programs?
What goals do you have for your toddler?
Do you have any questions for me?

Source: Adapted from Understanding Child Development (7th ed.), by R. Charlesworth, 2008, Clifton Park, NY: Thomson Delmar Learning.

Gathering information from families can help you ease separation difficulties and provide consistency. Some teachers use interview questions (see Table 1–23) in conversations, when conducting a home visit, or when parents come and go each day. Most parents enjoy talking about their children and feel reassured as you seek to understand their toddler. However, too many questions at one time can be overwhelming, so use good judgment and watch parents for cues on how comfortable they feel answering questions.

RECOMMENDED READINGS

Balaban, N. (2006). *Everyday goodbyes: Starting school and early care—a guide to the separation process.* Teachers College Press. (ISBN 08-8077-4639-8). Describes why children take time to adjust and the unpleasant feelings they experience. Includes classroom activities to increase children's feelings of independence and self-confidence. Cultural and special needs are also addressed.

Barker, A., & Manfredi-Petitt, L. (2004). *Relationships, the heart of quality care: Creating caring communities among adults in early care settings.* National Association for the Education of Young Children. (ISBN 1-928896-19-7). This book is full of profound ideas and strategies adults can implement to build strong, trusting relationships with one another.

Bergen, D., Torelli, L., & Reid, R. (2001). *Educating and caring for very young children: Infant/toddler curriculum.* Teachers College Press. (ISBN 0-8077-4010-1).

Edwards, C., & Gandini, L. (2001). *Bambini: The Italian approach to infant toddler care.* Teachers College Press. (ISBN 0-8077-4008-X).

Greenman, J., & Stonehouse, A. (1996). *Prime times: A handbook for excellence in infant toddler programs.* Redleaf Press. (ISBN 1-8848-3415-9). Outlines the process and goals for developing high-quality programs for young children. Forms, charts, and illustrations are included.

Isbell, R., & Isbell, C. (2003). *Learning spaces book for infants and toddlers.* Gryphon House. (ISBN 0-8765-9293-0). Create learning spaces unique for the needs of toddlers and infants. Includes more than 50 different learning spaces for four age groups of infants and toddlers.

RECOMMENDED WEB SITES

Dealing with Toddlers: http://www.urbanext.uiuc.edu. Offers ideas on managing common behavior and problems such as toileting, the need to explore, and negativism.

Parenting Babies and Toddlers: http://babyparenting.about.com. Includes tips for handling common concerns with infants and toddlers.

Toddlers Today: http://toddlerstoday.com. Provides information on toddler development and difficulties that may arise.

Also see "Recommended Web Sites" in the sections on infants and children ages three through six.

SUPPORTING THE DEVELOPMENT OF CHILDREN AGES THREE THROUGH SIX

Children ages three through six are actively involved in investigating and understanding the world. Development is shifting from sensory and motor activities to symbolic representation. Children are learning to make decisions and need adult guidance, but too much adult regulation may interfere with their ability to be self-directed. Supporting three- to six-year-olds means knowing when to step in and when to stand back. This chapter provides some strategies for supporting children while facilitating independence. It is organized by domains—physical, motor, cognitive, language, and social-emotional. Within each domain, patterns of development are described, and techniques for supporting development are suggested. At the end of the section, developmental alerts are identified and considerations for working with families are provided. If you are working with children ages three through six, you will also find it helpful to review the sections on toddlers and children ages six through eight.

PHYSICAL GROWTH

Healthy physical growth is the foundation for developing independence (see Table 1–24). Brain growth and maturation result in increased coordination between thoughts and actions, as planning and analyzing skills advance. Children's appetites decrease, and smaller appetites combined with the tendency to eat more processed foods and less nutrient-dense foods can threaten children's health by leading to misnourishment, malnutrition, and obesity. Misnourishment occurs when children's diets have an adequate amount of calories but lack adequate essential nutrients, whereas malnutrition occurs when children's diets are inadequate in both

TABLE 1—24 PHYSICAL GROWTH CHARACTERISTICS OF CHILDREN AGES THREE THROUGH SIX

Child's Name_____ Birth Date _____

Physical Growth	Date
3 years old	
Height increases 2 to 3 in. per year, avg. height is 38 to 40 in.	
Gains approximately 3 to 5 lb per year, avg. weight is 30 to 38 lb	
Has all baby teeth	
Appetite decreases	
Sleeps 10 to 12 hours per night; may wake early; may give up nap	
4 years old	
Height increases by approximately 2 in. per year; avg. height is 40 to 45 in.	
Weight increases by approximately 4 to 5 lb per year; avg. weight is 32 to 40 lb	
Appetite fluctuates	
Sleeps 10–12 hours night; might nap	
5 years old	
Height increases by approximately 2 in. per year; avg. height is 42 to 46 in.	
Weight increases by approximately 4 to 5 lb per year; avg. weight is 38 to 45 lb	
Head size is approximately size of adults	
May begin losing baby teeth	
Eats well most meals, but not always	
Sleeps 10 to 11 hours at night; might still nap	

Source: Adapted from *Developmental Profiles, Pre-Birth through Twelve* (5th ed.), by K. D. Allen & L. R. Marotz, 2007, Clifton Park, NY: Thomson Delmar Learning. Reprinted with permission of Delmar Learning, a division of Thomson Learning: http://www.thomsonrights.com Fax 800 730-2215.

nutrients and calories. If children have a weight that is low for their height, it may be a sign that they are misnourished. Children suffering from both misnourishment and malnutrition are susceptible to cognitive and health difficulties (Berger, 2005; Marcon, 2003).

Poor nutrition is also a contributing factor in obesity. Poor nutrition and a lack of physical activity both significantly contribute to higher rates of obesity among children. The American Academy of Pediatrics (AAP) (2003) reports that pediatric obesity has reached epidemic proportions and is increasing. Obese children are at greater risk for long-term health difficulties such as diabetes or orthopedic problems and may suffer psychologically if they are teased by peers (Charlesworth, 2008). It is likely that you will have children in your class who are struggling with these issues.

Your Role: Supporting Physical Growth

Children ages three through six are naturally curious and desire to learn about all parts of their bodies and how they function. This includes nutrition, exercise, health and hygiene, and genital organs. This is a prime time for education about nutrition, physical growth, health and hygiene, and bodily functions. Children's health remains vulnerable to diseases (cold, flu, chicken pox, etc.), accidents (car accidents, poisons, drowning), toxins (poisons, lead in water), maltreatment (abuse, neglect), and nutritional deficiencies. Your primary role is to prevent possible threats to children's health through educating parents and children, providing adequate supervision, implementing appropriate health and safety procedures, reporting maltreatment (see Appendix B), and providing a safe environment. Frequent hand washing and early identification of contagious illness continue to be hallmarks in promoting children's health (see Appendix A). The following information provides suggestions for helping children with issues surrounding nutrition, obesity, and masturbation.

Nutrition and Obesity

Children ages three through six have developed definite food preferences and usually prefer small servings. They need a balanced variety of food choices and need to be taught basic nutrition concepts (see http://www.mypyramid.gov). Nutrition education programs are most effective when parents are involved. Diets of young children are influenced by culture, religion, and the media. Respect family eating patterns and preferences, and try to accommodate them whenever possible (religious needs, vegetarian diets, etc.; see also http://www.semda.com). Encourage and provide opportunities for families to share cultural eating experiences with the class as appropriate. The media also influences children's diets. Ongoing daily discussions about appropriate nutrition choices are essential to prevent misconceptions. If you are concerned that a child is suffering from malnutrition or misnourishment, refer parents to a health care provider. Frequently, families of malnourished children have financial concerns. Be sensitive to this issue. Find out which resources can help families in your area. Your state's health department or department of human services are good places to find information. Make appropriate referrals and follow up to ensure that children's needs are being met.

Additionally, the AAP (2003) recommends that adults prevent childhood obesity by providing proper nutrition, facilitating gross motor activities several times a day, and avoiding the use of television in child care programs. To prevent obesity, total daily television and video game time should be limited to two hours per day. The U.S. Department of Agriculture (USDA) recommends that children participate in at least 60 minutes of physical activity every day (USDA, 2005). (See also "Motor Development" section for children ages six through eight.) The checklist in Table 1–25 includes diet recommendations for preventing childhood obesity and addressing nutrition concerns (see "Recommended Web Sites" for USDA teacher resources). Use the information you collect to set goals and improve professional practices.

Masturbation

Three- to six-year-olds are naturally curious and learning about all parts of their bodies and how they function. They may masturbate or participate in consensual exploration of sexual organs with same-age peers in a curious, playful manner. Though these are normal curiosities for children, genital organs, reproduction, and sexual privacy can be sensitive topics for teachers and parents. Parents are principally responsible for addressing these issues with their children and setting appropriate limits (Chrisman & Couchenour, 2002). However, some parents may be unsure of how to appropriately talk to young children about sexuality. You can support parents by providing accurate information and communicating openly about behaviors you see in the classroom. Masturbation is common up to the age of five or six. Most children need to be taught that masturbation is not a public activity. Frequent masturbation can be a sign of stress or neglect. Occasionally, it is an indicator of sexual abuse (see Appendix B; AAP, 2005e). If you are concerned about sexual abuse, report the situation to local authorities immediately. Keep in mind that it is normal for masturbation in private to continue depending on the culture and attitudes of parents. If masturbation becomes a problem, children should be seen by a physician (AAP, 2005e). Suggestions for appropriately handling masturbation include the following:

- Communicate to children that curiosity about all parts of their bodies is natural, but nudity and sexual play in public are not appropriate (AAP, 2005e).

- Teach children that unless a doctor or parent needs to examine them because of some type of pain in the genital area, no one else should touch their "private parts" (AAP, 2005e).

TABLE 1–25   SUPPORTING HEALTHY NUTRITION SELF-CHECKLIST

	Rarely	Sometimes	Frequently
I eat with children and model healthy, balanced food choices.			
I involve children in planning healthy meals and preparation of food (be sure to follow safe food preparation guidelines— check with local health department).			
I encourage children to regulate their own food intake by allowing them to choose portion sizes and make healthy choices.			
I provide whole grains for at least half of all grains offered to children.			
I provide a wide variety of vegetables, including dark green and orange vegetables.			
I provide calcium-rich foods including fat-free milk and yogurt several times a day (toddlers need whole milk products; infants need formula).			
I provide low-fat protein foods including beans, peas, nuts, chicken, turkey, or fish.			
I provide fruits for meals and snacks (only small amounts of juice).			
I avoid serving food and drinks with sugar and few nutrients.			
During mealtimes, I talk with children about the foods they are eating and the role each type of food has in helping our bodies function.			
I help children study the human body, how it functions, and the role of nutrition.			
I integrate nutrition concepts across the curriculum (play food, empty food boxes in dramatic play, books about food and nutrition, children sort food into food groups, etc.).			
I educate parents about appropriate nutrition for children (e.g., newsletters, bulletin boards, workshops; send-home articles; invite a nutritionist to speak at a parent night).			
In the space below, identify one goal for personal improvement and reevaluate your progress in three weeks. Goal:			

Source: Adapted from U.S. Department of Agriculture, "*Tips for Families,*" retrieved November 23, 2006, from http://teamnutrition.usda.gov

■ If children are masturbating in the classroom, approach this topic in a private, calm, matter-of-fact manner— children should not feel shame or humiliation (Chrisman & Couchenour, 2002). Explain that touching the private parts of their bodies is not appropriate in public. They may need a reminder to wash their hands after touching their genitals.

■ Give children quiet reminders to help them learn to control their impulses. Chrisman and Couchenour (2002) have found that reminding children about other things they can do with their hands (e.g., play with the play dough) and redirecting children to activities that interest them is an effective strategy.

■ If masturbation seems to be an outlet for anxiety or stress, identify the cause. If possible, change the stressor, or teach children alternate coping strategies (e.g., sensory play, physical activity, dramatic play, relaxation, etc.).

MOTOR DEVELOPMENT

Through motor skills children engage with the world. Developing motor skills helps children become more independent and meet challenges. During the preschool years, control of fundamental skills increases in speed and complexity (running, jumping, kicking, throwing, and catching). More complex skills including skipping, hopping, pedaling, and writing emerge and refine (see Table 1–26 on p. 80–81). Fine motor skills include the coordination of wrist and finger muscles, and also require hand-eye coordination. Fine motor skills are essential for writing and literacy (Schickedanz, 1999). The development of gross and fine motor skills contributes significantly to increases in cognitive, social, and language development. When children learn through movement, they remember things better. Movement can also help children learn to take the perspective of other people or things. When children pretend to move like a frog, climb to a higher platform, or hang upside down, they see the world in a different way. Movement also requires that children be aware of their body positioning in space, relative to other people and things (Pica, 1997). Delayed motor development limits children's ability to explore and investigate and can result in delays in other areas (e.g., social, cognitive, language).

Your Role: Supporting Motor Skills

Motor skill development follows a pattern. First children explore and practice new movements. As they learn what works well, coordination

TABLE 1—26   MOTOR DEVELOPMENT CHARACTERISTICS OF CHILDREN AGES THREE THROUGH SIX

Child's Name_____   Birth Date _____

Motor Development	Date
3 years old	
Gross motor	
Balances momentarily on one foot	
Kicks a large ball; catches a large bounced ball with both arms extended	
Jumps in place	
Enjoys swinging on a swing	
Pedals a small tricycle or Bigwheel	
Fine motor	
Beginning to show hand dominance	
Molds clay by pounding, squeezing, and rolling it	
Turns single pages of books	
Uses eight or more blocks to build a tower	
Self-help skills	
Carries a cup or glass of liquid with minimal spilling	
Needs little assistance to feed self	
Has bladder control	
Can manipulate large buttons and zippers on clothing	
Washes and dries hands	
Partially brushes own teeth	
4 years old	
Gross motor	
Walks a straight line (tape or chalk line on the floor)	
Hops on one foot	
Pedals and steers a wheeled toy with confidence; avoids obstacles and oncoming "traffic"	
Climbs ladders, trees, playground equipment	
Jumps over objects 5 or 6 inches (12.5 to 15 cm) high; lands with both feet together	
Throws a ball overhand	
Runs, starts, stops, and moves around obstacles with ease	

TABLE 1–26 MOTOR DEVELOPMENT CHARACTERISTICS OF CHILDREN AGES THREE THROUGH SIX (*Continued*)

Motor Development	Date
Fine motor	
Uses 10 or more blocks to build a tower	
Makes simple shapes out of clay such as snakes, cookies	
Threads wooden beads on a string	
Can hit pegs or nails with a hammer	
Uses tripod grip to hold a crayon or marker	
Self-help	
Takes care of toileting on own	
Dresses self—buttons, laces, buckles belts	
5 years old	
Gross motor	
Walks backward, heel to toe	
Walks unassisted up and down stairs, alternating feet	
Learns to turn somersaults (should be taught the right way in order to avoid injury)	
Touches toes without flexing knees	
Catches a ball thrown from 3 feet away	
Walks on a balance beam	
Learns to skip using alternating feet	
Catches ball thrown from 3 feet away	
Balances on either foot with good control for 10 seconds	
Jumps or hops forward 10 times in a row without falling	
Rides a tricycle or wheeled toy with speed and skillful steering; some learn to ride bicycles, usually with training wheels	
Fine motor	
Can reproduce shapes—triangle, square, and circle	
Can reproduce a three-dimensional model using small cubes	
Has good control of pencil or marker	
Has clearly established hand dominance	
Cuts on line with scissors	
Self-help	
Bathes, dresses, and takes care of toileting independently most of the time	

Source: Adapted from *Developmental Profiles, Pre-Birth through Twelve* (5th ed.), by K. D. Allen & L. R. Marotz, 2007, Clifton Park, NY: Thomson Delmar Learning. Reprinted with permission of Delmar Learning, a division of Thomson Learning: http://www.thomsonrights.com. Fax 800 730-2215.

improves and skills are refined. Finally, mastery is achieved and children use movements at will (Sutterby & Thornton, 2005). Your role in supporting the development of motor skills is to provide the time, space, instruction, and opportunities to help children engage in this process. The following information includes some basic ideas for facilitating the development of gross and fine motor skills.

Gross Motor Skills

Physical activity is critical for optimal development across all domains. However, most children's active play does not provide enough physical intensity. Your role is to plan a balance of structured and unstructured daily movement activities. Outdoor time provides rich opportunities for creative play and social cooperation (Sutterby & Thornton, 2005). Here are a few ideas for facilitating gross motor development.

- Go outside or to a gross motor area every day. Total daily physical activity for children should be at least one hour.

- Supervise children at all times.

- Plan specific activities (e.g., obstacle courses), or use movement songs and simple games (formal games with rules are not appropriate) to encourage children to participate in higher-intensity physical activity.

- Use teaching strategies that emphasize exploration of movement, body awareness, and coordination (using music, dance, etc.; Pica, 1997).

- Teach motor skills by breaking down movements into specific smaller steps, offering suggestions, and providing scaffolding for children (Charlesworth, 2008).

- To keep things interesting and help children remember concepts, integrate science, math, dramatic play, woodworking, and literacy activities into outdoor time or with music and movement. Examples include taking large blocks, dramatic play props, art easels, and the woodworking bench outside.

- Encourage children to use movement to explore concepts about things, and to explore new roles and pretend to be other people (Smith, 2002).

- Build movement vocabulary by asking children to describe their movements, and explain how to repeat movements.

Write down their descriptions, read them back to children, and encourage peers to try to repeat the movement (Smith, 2002).

■ Provide large areas on playgrounds that are wide, open, and flat to allow children freedom of movement (Sutterby & Thornton, 2005).

■ Include equipment for climbing, balancing, and development of upper-body strength (rings, monkey bars). Also provide slides, and swings that allow children to move through space in different ways (Sutterby & Thornton, 2005)

■ Make sure that the playground and equipment is accessible for all children, and that all children are physically able to participate to their full capabilities (Sutterby & Thornton, 2005).

■ Choose equipment that is challenging and provides an element of risk taking, yet meets safety standards (Sutterby & Thornton, 2005).

■ Provide a sand and water area with sand toys, buckets, funnels, small wagons, and wheelbarrows.

■ Interact with children by asking questions, making suggestions, teaching specific skills, and encouraging them to try new things.

■ Provide riding toys such as scooters, tricycles, and vehicles that can accommodate two or more children, as well as ramps and teeter-totters, to facilitate cooperation.

Fine Motor Skills

Small-muscle dexterity develops through practice with markers, puzzles, kitchen utensils, and paintbrushes. Hand-eye coordination develops as children build towers with blocks, paint, or hammer nails. Perceptual discrimination refines as children experiment with drawing and writing, observe art and environmental print, and have books read to them (Charlesworth, 2008).

Your role in helping children develop fine motor skills is to provide a variety of materials—and time—to explore. Individual children will prefer working with different sizes and types of manipulatives and a variety of writing and art materials. Provide a wide variety of options and allow them to choose. Children begin fine motor skill development by experimenting and becoming familiar with materials. Here are a few suggestions for materials to provide.

- self-help props including dress-up clothes and accessories for dramatic play with buttons and zippers, dressing boards, lacing cards, and kitchen utensils and dishes

- things to string including sewing boards, a variety of beads, and metal or plastic rings (e.g., from milk jugs or glass jars)

- things that move, such as small trucks and cars

- musical instruments—use them with movement activities to help children coordinate fine and gross motor skills

- construction manipulatives such as gear builders, snap cubes, bristle blocks, log builders, and pipe builders

- problem-solving manipulatives including a wide variety of table and floor puzzles, small items for sorting and counting, and pattern cards

- sensory materials and accessories such as sand and water with containers to pour, sift, and measure, as well as clay with tools for molding and shaping

- art supplies including scissors, a variety of paintbrushes, glue, tape, markers, crayons, watercolor paints, paper, feathers, pom-poms, wooden shapes, and so on. Designate a table and allow children to use this self-directed art center during free-choice time

- writing materials including a variety of pencils, markers, paper, and envelopes to fold and manipulate

- woodworking center with hammers, hand drills, nuts, bolts, saws, and safety gloves and goggles

COGNITIVE DEVELOPMENT

Young children love to learn and investigate. Preschoolers may frequently ask "Why?" as they attempt to understand the world through cause-and-effect relationships. The thinking of preschoolers is more magical than logical. They tend to attribute human characteristics to objects (e.g., the toy feels sad) or see things solely from their own perspective (e.g., the ocean exists for me to swim in). However, cognitive processes are becoming more logical and activities such as sorting, classifying, counting, patterning, and putting things in order from largest to smallest provide a foundation for logical thinking and math concepts. Between the ages of five and seven, children begin to transition to more complex logical thinking. You can observe this change in thinking as children begin to demonstrate the understanding that a person or thing can belong to more than one category (a puppy may be an animal, a dog, and a poodle; their teacher may also be a mommy), or when they recognize that even though the shape of a ball of clay, size of a glass of water, or length of a row of pennies has changed, the amount has not (i.e., *conservation*, see Table 1–27; Piaget & Inhelder, 1969).

TABLE 1–27 COGNITIVE DEVELOPMENT CHARACTERISTICS OF CHILDREN AGES THREE THROUGH SIX

Child's Name_____   Birth Date _____

Cognitive Development	Date
3 years old	
Plays realistically: feeds doll; hooks truck and trailer together	
Places 8 to 10 pegs in pegboard, or 6 round and 6 square blocks in form board	
Identifies shapes	
Matches and names red, yellow, blue	
Counts objects	
4 years old	
Stacks at least five graduated cubes largest to smallest; builds a pyramid of six blocks	
Knows the concepts of *biggest, tallest, same, more*	
Counts to 20 or more	
Likes stories about how things grow and operate	
Understands daily sequence of events	
5 years old	
Identifies position of object—first, second, last	
Builds steps with set of small blocks	
Understands concepts of same shape, same size	
Sorts objects on the basis of two dimensions, such as color and form	
Sorts objects so that all things in the group have a single common feature	
Understands smallest and shortest; places objects in order from shortest to tallest, smallest to largest	

Source: Adapted from *Developmental Profiles, Pre-Birth through Twelve* (5th ed.), by K. D. Allen & L. R. Marotz, 2007, Clifton Park, NY: Thomson Delmar Learning. Reprinted with permission of Delmar Learning, a division of Thomson Learning: http://www.thomsonrights.com. Fax 800 730-2215.

Your Role: Supporting Cognitive Development

Young children learn in a variety of ways, including through verbal interactions, music, movement, nature and science explorations, art, hands-on play with objects, and social relationships. Individual children have unique learning preferences and need opportunities to explore how they learn best. They are learning how to solve problems, think about problems, and use problem-solving vocabulary. They need daily opportunities to sort, classify, count, and order things using a variety of materials (e.g., glass stones, plastic lids, coins, people, animals, etc.). Play continues to be the best method for engaging children in multiple types of learning and creating a sense of discovery. Creativity emerges as children have opportunities to master concepts and skills, then apply understandings in novel ways.

Your role is to provide a stimulating environment and guide their investigations through individual, meaningful interactions. One tool for this is to ask children open-ended, thought-provoking questions. Open-ended questions encourage creative thinking. Examples include "How is ice made?" or "How can we change water?" These types of questions promote creative thinking. Listen to and watch children carefully to learn about how their thinking is developing. Then use the information you collect to construct a curriculum that will be meaningful (see Table 1–28).

Technology is often used to help support cognitive development. However, some software programs stimulate thinking skills, whereas others are based only on rote memorization and may not be appropriate for young children. Adult guidance and supervision is an important element of using technology in the classroom. Technology should also be balanced with other activities and overuse should be avoided (see "Recommended Web Sites" for more information; Early Connections, 2006). Early Connections recommends that appropriate software should

- connect concepts with things children already know.
- support curriculum goals.
- facilitate exploration and problem solving.
- allow children to govern the pace.

LANGUAGE DEVELOPMENT

Language develops from simple sounds without meaning to meaningful sounds, words, and sentences. To master language,

TABLE 1—28   MEANINGFUL LEARNING SELF-CHECKLIST

	Yes	No
I actively observe and listen to children, collecting information about things that interest them.		
I actively engage children in the planning process by helping them identify what they already know and what they want to learn.		
I choose topics for study that help children better understand themselves, others, and their environment and relate to children's real-life experiences.		
I allow individual children to explore interests other than the topics I have chosen, and extend the individual interests and learning preferences of children.		
I provide materials and props that children can touch, see, hear, taste, or smell.		
I provide real-life experiences connected to the interests of children, including experiments, expert guests, and field trips.		
I provide multiple ways for children to explore and understand concepts (blocks, art, dramatic play, music and movement, literacy, manipulatives and mathematical explorations, science experiments, etc.)		
I plan ways for children to document their learning and share it with others (make books, parent night presentation, bulletin board, etc.)		
I ask children questions that encourage investigation and problem solving: "What do you notice about . . .?", "What else would you like to learn about . . . .?", "What would happen if . . .?", "Why do you think_____happens?", "How could you make that work . . .?", "Can you think of another way to make that work?"		
I model questioning, thinking strategies, and problem-solving skills.		
I encourage children to talk about what they are thinking by asking questions such as "How did you think of that?"		
I provide ample time in the daily schedule for children to choose different methods of learning and pursue individual interests.		
After self-evaluating, set one goal to work on for the next month:		

Source: Adapted from Tools of the Mind: The Vygotskian Approach to Early Childhood Education. by E. Bodrova & D. J. Leong, 1996, Englewood Cliffs, NJ: Merrill/Prentice Hall; and Young Investigators: The Project Approach in the Early Years, by J. H. Helm & L. Katz, 2001, New York: Teachers College Press and National Association for the Education of Young Children.

children must learn how to combine small sounds (e.g., "br" or "kl") and longer sounds (e.g., "pre" and "ing") in meaningful ways to make words. They also must learn to combine words into phrases or sentences that make sense. Culture, environment, and biology all seem to influence this process. Families not only teach children language skills, but also how to use those skills. How families use language varies due to differences in ethnic group, socioeconomic status, culture, and religious beliefs. Some families emphasize reading for pleasure; others emphasize reading for information. Some use language to communicate feelings; others emphasize the communication of information. Many times, language dialects that are not Standard English serve important functions in children's home environments. It is important for teachers to encourage English language development while allowing for individual differences. Providing a language-rich environment where children are engaged in conversations and print activities supports this process. By four years old, most children have acquired most oral language abilities. However, they still tend to understand and use words literally and may not realize when they have incomplete information or misconceptions (Charlesworth, 2008; Schickedanz, 1999).

At about age three, children become interested in writing names and pretend to write cursive. Through exploration, loops, curves, and lines develop into recognizable letters. Children begin putting letters in the right order and eventually recognize that letters represent an oral sound. Children experiment with this principle by identifying the starting sounds of a word, then the ending sound, and eventually learn to discriminate the sounds in between (may not be until kindergarten or later). By age six, children may capitalize the first letter of their name and experiment with writing a variety of words. Repetition of letters and words, and letter reversals (b, d, s, p, q) are common and indicate that children are discovering how language works (Schickedanz & Casbergue, 2004). See Table 1–29 for a review of language development characteristics.

Your Role: Supporting Language Development

Language helps children communicate, build relationships, and learn cultural expectations (Owocki, 2001). Because young children understand more language than they can speak, listening to them and engaging in meaningful conversations with them is the best method for facilitating language development. Talking with them about thoughts and feelings improves self-understanding.

Children also enjoy using language in playful ways (e.g., "Name Game" song) or simple jokes that play on words. Your role in supporting children's language development is to engage children in meaningful conversations, provide support for emerging writing and reading skills, and identify delays in the acquisition of

TABLE 1–29   LANGUAGE DEVELOPMENT CHARACTERISTICS OF CHILDREN AGES THREE THROUGH SIX

Child's Name_____   Birth Date _____

Language	Date
3 years old	
Listens attentively and makes relevant comments during age-appropriate stories, especially those related to home and family events	
Likes to look at books and may pretend to "read" to others or explain pictures	
Enjoys stories with riddles, guessing, and suspense	
Points with fair accuracy to correct pictures when given sound-alike words: keys—cheese; fish—dish; mouse—mouth	
Talks about objects, events, and people not present: "Jerry has a pool in his yard"	
Talks about the actions of others: "Daddy's mowing the grass"	
Adds information to what has just been said: "Yeah, and then he grabbed it back"	
Answers simple questions appropriately	
Asks increasing numbers of questions, including location/identity of objects and people	
Uses increased speech forms to keep conversation going: "What did he do next?" "How come she hid?"	
Uses markers, or crayons to create vertical, horizontal, and circular marks	
4 years old	
Uses the prepositions "on," "in," and "under"	
Uses possessives consistently: "hers," "theirs," "baby's"	
Indicates if paired words sound the same or different: sheet-feet, ball-wall	
Answers "Whose?" "Who?" "Why?" and "How many?"	
Produces elaborate sentence structures	
Uses almost entirely intelligible speech	
Begins to correctly use the past tense of verbs: "Mommy closed the door," "Daddy went to work"	
Is able to draw some shapes and write some letters	
5 years old	
Has vocabulary of 1,500 words or more	
Tells a familiar story while looking at pictures in a book	
Uses functional definitions: a ball is to bounce; a bed is to sleep in	
Identifies and names four to eight colors	

(Continued)

TABLE 1–29   LANGUAGE DEVELOPMENT CHARACTERISTICS OF CHILDREN AGES THREE THROUGH SIX (*Continued*)

Language	Date
5 years old	
Recognizes the humor in simple jokes; makes up jokes and riddles	
Produces sentences with five to seven words; much longer sentences are not unusual	
Reproduces some letters—typically from own name	

Source: Adapted from *Developmental Profiles, Pre-Birth through Twelve* (5th ed.), by K. D. Allen & L. R. Marotz, 2007, Clifton Park, NY: Thomson Delmar Learning. Reprinted with permission of Delmar Learning, a division of Thomson Learning: http://www.thomsonrights.com. Fax 800 730-2215.

skills (see information for English language learners in the "Special Needs" section). The following information provides suggestions for supporting reading and writing.

Reading

Children need authentic literacy activities that fit their learning style and that are meaningful to them. Group instruction or drill-and-practice activities are not as meaningful for young children and should be avoided (International Reading Association [IRA] & NAEYC, 1999). There are several methods for teaching reading. Most follow either a whole-language approach or a phonics approach. Whole-language methods view children as actively involved in learning—reading, writing, spelling, and grammar are seen as a whole and are taught with an integrated approach. Literacy learning takes place in learning centers that are based on meaningful life experiences or study topics. Children write about personal experiences and thoughts. Phonics approaches focus on teaching children letter recognition, sounds, and word patterns. These approaches are usually teacher directed and lack connections to everyday language uses. Many teachers find that both approaches have benefits for children, and that using both in meaningful ways is most beneficial.

Appropriate goals can help guide your decisions. Schickedanz (1999) suggests that preschoolers should be able to enjoy and tell stories (see Table 1–31 for recommended books), attempt to read and write, rhyme, and connect some sounds with letters. As they gain maturity and experience, children should be able to retell a simple story, identify most letters and sounds, track print from left to right, and write names and small familiar words.

Use the self-evaluation in Table 1–30 to help you reflect upon your teaching practices for helping children develop reading skills. You may also ask a peer to observe you for additional feedback. Table 1–31 includes a list of suggested authors and readings for children ages three through six.

Writing

Writing emerges from drawing. Encourage children to draw and experiment with writing materials. Children ages three through

TABLE 1–30 SUPPORTING READING DEVELOPMENT SELF-CHECKLIST

	Rarely	Sometimes	Frequently
I help children recognize that printed words have meaning by reading everyday printed materials aloud (e.g., books, labels, signs, newspapers, lesson plans, notes from parents, recipes).			
I play games that encourage children to find letters of the alphabet or logos in printed material.			
I use songs, games, and conversations to help children associate sounds with letters.			
I use nursery rhymes, and help children make their own rhymes, to develop awareness of sound patterns.			
I make labels for objects and materials in the classroom. I include a picture of the item next to the word on the label, and place a matching label on the shelf where the item belongs, to help children return things independently.			
I read the children's favorite books repeatedly. I encourage their attempts to "read" the books and predict events.			
I ask children questions relating to the story before beginning reading: "What do you know about trains?" or "Have you ever ridden on a train?" After we finish the book, I ask questions such as "What surprised you about this story?" or "What was your favorite part?"			
I relate stories to children's past experiences.			
I model writing with purpose during everyday activities. I print the words for songs. I write down things children say (responses to questions, etc.).			
I teach children that stories have a beginning, middle, and end. I help them identify these components after reading a story. I ask questions such as "How did this story start?"			

(Continued)

TABLE 1–30 SUPPORTING READING DEVELOPMENT SELF-CHECKLIST (*Continued*)			
	Rarely	**Sometimes**	**Frequently**
I provide books of all kinds: picture books, realistic stories, alphabet books, poetry, and informational books.			
I spend time reading with children individually.			
I encourage children to use books to solve everyday problems and answer questions they have: "What kind of bug is that?" or "How do cars work?"			
Identify one goal for personal improvement and revaluate in two weeks.			
Goal:			

Source: Adapted from *Learning to Read and Write: Developmentally Appropriate Practices for Young Children,* International Reading Association & the National Association for the Education of Young Children, 1999, Washington, DC: NAEYC; and *Much More Than the ABC's: The Early Stages of Reading and Writing,* by J. A. Schickedanz, 1999, Washington, DC: NAEYC.

six will make letter-like marks, repeat letter patterns, make marks from left to right, write lists of letters, and notice similarities and differences in words (Owocki, 2001). Letter reversals, repetition, incorrect order, and inventive spelling are common. Teachers and parents may become concerned that children will learn to spell things incorrectly if their initial inventive spelling is not correct. However, most children refine spelling skills as their experience and knowledge increases (Schickedanz & Casbergue, 2004).

Remember to keep the focus on the progress children are making, rather than the product. The most important thing is that children enjoy writing. Use the self-evaluation in Table 1–32 (see p. 94) to reflect upon teaching practices that facilitate the development of writing skills. You may also ask a peer to observe your abilities, then provide additional feedback. The information you collect can be used to set goals and improve your professional practices. Schickedanz and Casbergue (2004) suggest the following strategies for helping children connect language and writing (see also "Motor Development" section).

- Make a journal for each child by stapling blank paper together. Construction paper may be used as the cover. Children can make an entry each day by drawing pictures, dictating stories, and writing words they know.

TABLE 1–31 SUGGESTED AUTHORS AND BOOKS FOR CHILDREN AGES THREE THROUGH SIX

Audrey Wood

The Napping House

Ten Little Fish

Piggies

Sweet Dream Pies

Jon Agee

Terrific

Jan Brett

The Mitten

The Umbrella

Honey...Honey...Lion

The Hat

Gingerbread Boy

Margie Palatini

Piggy Pie

Zoom Broom

Audrey Penn

The Kissing Hand

A Pocket Full of Kisses

David Shannon

A Bad Case of Stripes

No David

David Goes to School

Oh David

Margaret Wild

Our Granny

The Relatives Came

Wilford Gordon McDonald Partridge

- Encourage children to make books, cards, letters, and notes to peers and family.

- Encourage children to describe things (movements, people, animals, etc.) and write down their descriptions.

TABLE 1–32   SUPPORTING WRITING SELF-EVALUATION

Identify one example of how you implement the following criteria to support writing.

1. Recognize inventive spelling as a developmental process. Respond positively to children's attempts to spell words.

2. Teach children about the parts of the book, including cover, spine, title page, and end pages.

3. Teach children writing vocabulary including *author, illustrator,* and *editing.*

4. Take dictation from children and model writing skills. Verbalize the decisions you make while writing. "Sarah is a name so I need to capitalize the 'S.' That means the 'S' is larger than the other letters."

5. Read children's dictation; encourage them to "read" or repeat their dictation.

6. Encourage children to use writing to communicate and resolve problems. For example, have children write a note to parents about what they would like in their lunch the next day, or to a peer who has hurt their feelings.

7. Integrate writing in other areas of the curriculum (e.g., road signs for the block area, creat menus for dramatic play, write stories about artwork).

8. Provide examples of writing and letters in the environment so that children can look at and refer to them (alphabet charts, word walls, etc.).

9. Connect literacy learning with home by involving families in culturally appropriate open-ended activities they can do at home (e.g., for child's birthday, ask families to make a simple book about the day the child was born).

Evaluate which skills you have mastered and identify one area in which you would like to improve.

Source: Adapted from *Writing in Preschool: Learning to Orchestrate Meaning and Marks,* by J. A. Schickedanz & R. M. Casbergue, 2004, Newark, DE: International Reading Association; and *Learning to Read and Write: Developmentally Appropriate Practices for Young Children,* International Reading Association & the National Association for the Education of Young Children, 1999, Washington, DC: NAEYC.

- Play variations of games such as "I spy." Tell children you spy something that begins with an alphabet sound, and have them try to guess what it is.

- Have children sort pictures according to beginning sounds.

- Encourage children to write their own names on their art or projects. They might begin by writing only the first letter. You can extend this activity by having children tell you about their drawing and writing down what they say.

- Extend children's dramatic or block play by helping them write a script for a play that can be performed.

- Hang a magnetic white board in the room. Provide dry erase markers or magnetic letters for children to practice writing, drawing, and spelling.

- Encourage children to write letters with their fingers in sand, or use small boxes with salt in the bottom.

- Create a writing center with a variety of paper, pencils, alphabet stickers and stamps, and envelopes that children may choose from. Add novel materials such as clipboards, colored pencils, old calendars, envelopes, notepads, stationery, rubber stamps and ink pads, rulers, magnetic letters, stencil shapes, stickers, file cards, and office materials weekly to stimulate interest.

SOCIAL-EMOTIONAL DEVELOPMENT

Children ages three through six are active participants in creating their own relationships. Children experience a wide variety of emotional responses and need to recognize and control emotions in order to maintain relationships with others. Emotional attachments are broadening to include friends, teachers, and relatives (see Table 1–33). To play cooperatively, children must negotiate conflicts with peers. This helps them learn to see the perspective of others. Through play, children explore and test social-emotional abilities. They experiment with gender roles, emotions, and relationships with others. With maturity, social skills such as taking turns become easier as children recognize that rules apply to themselves as well as others. Making choices and experiencing the results allows children to learn about the effects of their actions. Respectful, genuine treatment and support from teachers on a daily basis are crucial for healthy emotional development (Charlesworth, 2008).

TABLE 1—33   SOCIAL-EMOTIONAL DEVELOPMENT CHARACTERISTICS OF CHILDREN AGES THREE THROUGH SIX

Child's Name_____   Birth Date _____

Social-Emotional Development	Date
3 years old	
Seems to understand taking turns, but not always willing to do so	
Laughs frequently; is friendly and eager to please	
Has occasional nightmares and fears the dark, monsters, and/or fire	
Joins in simple games and group activities, sometimes hesitantly	
Talks to self often	
Uses objects symbolically in play: block of wood may be a truck, a ramp, a bat	
4 years old	
Is outgoing and friendly; overly enthusiastic at times	
Changes moods rapidly and unpredictably; often throws tantrum over minor frustrations; sulks over being left out	
Holds conversations and shares strong emotions with imaginary playmates or companions; invisible friends are common	
Boasts, exaggerates, and "bends" the truth with made-up stories or claims; tests limits with "bathroom" talk	
Cooperates with others; participates in group activities	
Shows pride in accomplishments; seeks frequent adult approval	
5 years old	
Enjoys friendships; often has one or two special playmates	
Shares toys, takes turns, plays cooperatively (with occasional lapses); is often quite generous	
Participates in play and activities with other children; suggests imaginative and elaborate play ideas	
Is affectionate and caring, especially toward younger or injured children and animals	
Usually follows directions and carries out assignments; generally does what parent or teacher requests	
Continues to need adult comfort and reassurance, but may be less open in seeking and accepting comfort	

Source: Adapted from *Developmental Profiles, Pre-Birth through Twelve* (5th ed.), by K. D. Allen & L. R. Marotz, 2007, Clifton Park, NY: Thomson Delmar Learning. Reprinted with permission of Delmar Learning, a division of Thomson Learning: http://www.thomsonrights.com. Fax 800 730-2215.

Your Role: Supporting Social-Emotional Development

Self-regulation of emotions and social interactions is vital to healthy development. Your role is to spend time during everyday situations spontaneously teaching children how to invite others to play, comfort a hurt peer, and express feelings appropriately. Although children are becoming more independent, they still need adult support and guidance. Your role is a delicate balance of providing support for children while encouraging them to be independent and helping them function as a community. Children's growing independence can be supported by giving them opportunities to do things for themselves and others, providing choices that are more complex (yet still appropriate for children), and encouraging them to work cooperatively with others.

Diverse experiences and backgrounds will impact how individual children emotionally react to classroom expectations. Minority children may have a greater need for support. It is important for self-concept development that the values and beliefs of their families are not overwhelmed by the larger majority culture. You can support all children in your class by learning about their cultures, involving parents, and avoiding stereotyped behaviors and materials. Your role is to communicate to children that their feelings are accepted and normal, but that they must express feelings appropriately (Charlesworth, 2008, see also "Supporting Diverse Families" section). At the core of your ability to support children's social-emotional development are your beliefs and your ability to reflect honestly upon your practices.

Most of us are unaware of when our own attitudes and actions are biased or rejecting. Use the worksheet in Table 1–34 to reflect upon your teaching. To get a fresh perspective, ask a colleague to observe in your classroom using the same criteria and give you feedback. The following information provides a few tips on selecting guidance strategies.

Guidance

One of the most important decisions you make is choosing discipline techniques. Blair (2003) notes that children need to develop the ability to regulate emotions and attention in order to succeed in school. A perplexing variety of discipline methods and classroom management strategies are available. Additionally, almost everyone (parents, administrators, colleagues) has an opinion on what

TABLE 1–34   SUPPORTING SOCIAL-EMOTIONAL DEVELOPMENT

Supporting Social-Emotional Development

During the next few weeks, look over this list before beginning each day and choose one of the criteria to work on. At the end of the day, record one example of how you met that criterion. When you complete the worksheet, evaluate which criteria were difficult for you and which you are strongest in. Use the information for setting long-term goals.

1. I discuss and give reasons for limits and expectations.

2. I help children express anger constructively (examples might include writing or drawing).

3. I model reflective thinking strategies by verbalizing my thinking processes.

4. I help children learn to recognize facial cues of others and respond in a respectful, caring manner.

5. I build cooperative relationships with children by showing respect for their thoughts, ideas, and emotions.

6. I acknowledge and accept both positive and negative feelings.

7. I appreciate and value each child as a unique individual.

8. I observe children's play. I briefly interact with them to extend and enrich play without directing or dominating it.

9. I encourage all children to participate equally in activities.

10. I avoid gender, ethnic, and cultural stereotypes.

11. I respect the culture, customs, and behaviors of children.

12. I coach children in appropriate social skills and directly teach appropriate social skills.

13. I provide open-ended activities where children cannot fail, including sensory play, creative arts, and dramatic play.

Source: Adapted from *Understanding Child Development* (7th ed.), by R. Charlesworth, 2008, Clifton Park, NY: Thomson Delmar Learning; and *Guidance of Young Children* (6th ed.), by M. Marion, 2002, New York.

methods are appropriate and work best. When choosing a discipline method, keep in mind that a positive, respectful relationship with children is your most important resource in facilitating self-regulation. Time-out is often used, yet can result in children being singled out and leave them feeling humiliated. Take time to see things from the child's perspective, and use only methods that increase children's feelings of emotional security (Charlesworth, 2008). Other things to consider when choosing discipline methods include the following:

- The developmental characteristics of young children— children have limited experience and difficulty in transferring behaviors to new situations. They need to be taught appropriate behavior and must be given opportunities to practice.

- Children need to feel competent, accepted, and respected. Methods that take control from children, or single children out, undermine these needs. Methods that encourage children to function as much as possible on their own, and teach children what to do, build competence and understanding.

- Methods that shame, humiliate, and physically or emotionally harm children are not only inappropriate, they are unethical for early childhood professionals (see "Code of Ethical Conduct" section).

Induction techniques preserve children's sense of dignity by reasoning *with* them, explaining consequences, and teaching children appropriate behavior. These methods require patience and are most effective when based on a respectful relationship. Other suggestions from Marion (2002) include:

- Provide accurate feedback to children about their behavior. Accurate feedback includes acknowledging the accomplishments of children and being direct and honest when behavior is inappropriate.

- Clearly communicate appropriate expectations and consequences. Appropriate expectations include that children treat all people (including themselves) and property with respect. Teach children what they should do rather than focusing on "don't."

- Model appropriate behavior and communication skills.

- Evaluate the physical environment. Children need adequate space to prevent crowding, but not so much space they feel out of control. They need places to be alone, and to work with others. They need a predictable, organized environment where they can function independently. Children need environments that are novel and interesting but not overstimulating.

DEVELOPMENTAL ALERTS

Children ages three through six may have a variety of special needs, ranging from developmental delays to emotional difficulties. Early detection of special needs and appropriate intervention continue to be key aspects of supporting children's development. Children need to be evaluated by a health professional or child development specialist if

By the fourth birthday, the child

- does not use intelligible speech most of the time; have children's hearing checked if there is any reason for concern.

- does not understand and follow simple commands and directions.

- is unable to state own name and age.

- does not enjoy playing near or with other children.

- cannot use three- to four-word sentences.

- does not ask questions.

- cannot stay with an activity for three or four minutes; cannot play alone for several minutes at a time.

- cannot jump in place without falling.

- is unable to balance on one foot, at least briefly.

- does not help with dressing self.

By the fifth birthday, the child

- is unable to state own name in full.

- cannot recognize simple shapes: circle, square, triangle.

- struggles with catching a large ball when bounced (have child's vision checked).

- has difficulty speaking so as to be understood by strangers (have child's hearing checked).

- does not have good control of posture and movement.

- is unable to hop on one foot.

- does not appear interested in, and responsive to, surroundings.

- cannot respond to statements without constantly asking to have them repeated.

- is unable to dress self with minimal adult assistance— manage buttons, zippers.

- does not take care of own toilet needs—a five-year-old should have good bowel and bladder control with infrequent accidents.

Adapted from *Developmental Profiles, Pre-Birth Through Twelve* (5th ed.), by K. D. Allen & L. R. Marotz, 2007. Reprinted with permission of Delmar Learning, a division of Thomson Learning: http://www.thomsonrights.com. Fax 800 730-2215.

SUPPORTING FAMILIES OF CHILDREN AGES THREE THROUGH SIX

Families of three- to six-year-olds have diverse values, cultures, religions, and interaction patterns, yet all need to be understood and accepted. Your role is to help a diverse group of adults and children function as a community. Strong parent–child attachment relationships remain critical for preschoolers.

You can be the catalyst that helps families and children connect. You can provide education to help parents understand developmental characteristics, appropriate expectations, and opportunities for families to connect with one another (see "Supporting Diverse Families" section for more information). The questions in Table 1–35 may be used to gather information about families and deepen your understanding of their needs. You might also use some of these questions to create a questionnaire that parents can fill out and you can keep on file. Most parents enjoy talking about their children and receiving support. However, too many questions at one time can feel overwhelming—use good judgment and watch parents' reactions to see if they are comfortable about answering questions.

TABLE 1–35   CHILDREN AGES THREE THROUGH SIX FAMILY QUESTIONNAIRE

Children Three Through Six Family Questionnaire
What are your goals for your child?
What are your child's strengths?
What type of discipline do you use?
How does your child usually respond?
What types of activities does your child enjoy?
How does your child express anger?
Does your child play with any other children? If yes, what are their ages and how often?
Does your child have any difficulties interacting with peers?
What television programs and video or computer game does your child view-use? How frequently?
Does your child enjoy reading? Does your child show an interest in printed materials? How?
Does your child write or draw at home? If yes, what does your child write? What does your child draw?
Does your child show an interest in counting or numbers?
Are their any special considerations you would like me to know about?
Does your child have or has your child had any health concerns such as allergies?

RECOMMENDED READINGS

Chrisman, K., & Couchenour, D. (2002). *Healthy sexuality development: A guide for early childhood educators and families.* NAEYC. (ISBN 1-928896-05-7). Provides practical guidance about teaching children about sexuality and how to respond to behaviors related to sexual development.

Cox, A., & West, S. (2004). *Literacy play: Over 300 dramatic play activities that teach pre-reading skills.* Gryphon House. (ISBN 0876592922). Forty dramatic play ideas are described, including literacy objectives, materials, reproducible props, and bookmaking patterns.

Curtis, D., & Carter, M. (2003). *Designs for living and learning: Transforming early childhood classrooms.* Rodleaf Press. (ISBN 1929610297). Provides hundreds of wonderful photographs and a multitude of stimulating ideas for creating classrooms that nurture children and support their learning.

Evans, B. (2001). *You can't come to my birthday party!: Conflict resolution skills with young chidlren*. High Scope Press. (ISBN 1573791598). Six-step model is provided for resolving conflicts, and is applied to real-life classroom situations.

Heidemann, S., & Hewitt, D. (1992). *Pathways to play: Developing play skills in young children*. Redleaf Press. (ISBN 0934140650). Critical social skills for engaging in cooperative play are identified and strategies for fostering children's development are included. Assessment and planning forms are provided.

Helm, J. H., & Katz, L. (2001). *Young investigators: The project approach in the early years*. Teachers College Press. (ISBN 0-8077-4016-0). Ways to implement child-focused projects to engage young learners are presented. Includes planning sheets and practical solutions.

Hoffman, E. (2004). *Magic capes, amazing powers*. Redleaf Press. (ISBN 1929610475). Provides practical ideas for constructively redirecting superhero play.

Kaiser, B., & Rasminsky, J. S. (2006). *Challenging behavior in young children* (2nd ed.). Allyn and Bacon. (ISBN 0205493335). Focuses on out-of-control behaviors. Addresses how children use inappropriate strategies to meet personal needs and what adults can do to help children succeed.

McCracken, J. B., (Ed.). (1985). *Reducing stress in the lives of young children*. NAEYC. (ISBN 0-935989-03-X). This is a collection of strategies from numerous professionals. Contents include coping with issues such as death, separation, hospitalization, and crisis. A section on strengthening families and avoiding stress in the classroom is also included.

Schickedanz, J. A., & Casbergue, R. (2004). *Writing in preschool: Learning to orchestrate meaning and marks*. International Reading Association. (ISBN 0-87207-546-X). This book documents the development of children's writing. You will learn to identify key components in children's writing and enhance their development.

RECOMMENDED WEB SITES

Association for Childhood Education International (ACEI): http://www.acei.org. This Web site provides international information concerning young children. The ACEI has issued several position statements, including "*The Child's Right to Creative Thought and Expression.*" The ACEI addresses violence, war, obesity, brain development, and testing in early childhood. It also provides global guidelines for care and a self-assessment tool.

Early Connections: Technology in Early Childhood: http://www.netc.org. Provides information on technology and early childhood.

Society for Nutrition and Education: http://www.sne.org/. This is a professional organization that provides information on nutrition.

Southeastern Michigan Dietetic Association (SEMDA): http://www.semda.com. Includes culturally relevant food guides such as Arab, Chinese, Mexican, Cuban, Indian, and Native American.

TechLearn: http://www.techlearning.com. Provides reviews of software programs and support for educators.

The Project Approach: http://www.project-approach.com. Provides resources on the project approach.

United States Department of Agriculture: http://www.mypyramid.gov. Information including computer games for children and lesson plans for teachers are available from the USDA.

SUPPORTING THE DEVELOPMENT OF CHILDREN AGES SIX THROUGH EIGHT

Children ages six through eight are active, inquisitive, and eager to learn new skills. Logical thought is advancing and activities that require children to exercise newfound skills provide motivation. Social and language abilities are growing. Most children learn to read, and this opens a new way for them to learn independently. A great deal of children's time is spent at school, where cognitive development is emphasized. This often results in less time for the development of social and motor skills. However, these skills are not only critical for improved cognitive functioning, they are also imperative for future well-being. This section will address these developmental issues. It is organized by domains—physical, motor, cognitive, language, and social-emotional development. Within each domain patterns of development are described and techniques are suggested to support development. At the end of this section, developmental alerts are identified and considerations for working with families of primary-aged children are provided. The "Children Ages Three through Six" section also has information that applies to primary-aged children, and will be helpful to review.

PHYSICAL GROWTH

During this time frame, physical growth continues steadily and gender differences become more apparent (see Table 1–36). Boys are usually taller and weigh more than girls. However, by age seven some girls are taller. Physical growth of the brain slows significantly, but advances in the complexity and speed of higher-level thinking skills continue (Berger, 2005). Children are becoming independent at maintaining personal hygiene and making health decisions.

TABLE 1–36　PHYSICAL GROWTH CHARACTERISTICS OF CHILDREN AGES SIX THROUGH EIGHT

Child's Name_____　　Birth Date _____

Physical Growth	Date
6 years old	
Height increases by 2 to 3 in.; girls' avg. height is 42 to 46 in.; boys' avg. height is 44 to 47 in.	
Gains 5 to 7 lb per year; girls' avg. weight is 38 to 47 lb; boys' avg. weight is 42 to 49 lb	
Body appears lanky, and arms and legs grow rapidly	
Losing baby teeth; secondary teeth erupting	
Good appetite, may want second helpings; occasionally skips a meal	
Sleeps 9 to 11 hours at night	
7 years old	
Gains about 6 lb per year; average weight 50 to 55 lb	
Height gains average 2 to 3 in.	
Energy level fluctuates	
Baby teeth continue to be replaced by permanent teeth	
Sleeps 10 to 11 hours at night	
8 years old	
Gains 5 to 7 lb per year; average 55 to 61 lb; girls usually weight less than boys	
Height increase averages 2 to 3 in. per year	
Some girls may begin menses, develop breasts and pubic hair	
Has good appetite; boys usually eat more than girls	
Sleeps about 10 hours at night	

Source: Adapted from *Developmental Profiles, Pre-Birth through Twelve* (5th ed.), by K. D. Allen & L. R. Marotz, 2007, Clifton Park, NY: Thomson Delmar Learning. Reprinted with permission of Delmar Learning, a division of Thomson Learning: http://www.thomsonrights.com. Fax 800 730-2215.

Proper nutrition and physical activity continue to be critical for growth and energy requirements, as malnutrition and obesity pose serious threats to the health of children (see "Physical Growth" section for children ages three through six).

Your Role: Supporting Physical Growth

Because children are at school all day you may be the first to notice health difficulties. Changes in a child's appearance, behavior, or mood can indicate a problem. Early identification of illness, health difficulties, or maltreatment and appropriate health interventions are critical to healthy development (see Appendices A and B).

Some parents may need assistance in locating support systems for health care or obtaining food. Familiarize yourself with local services such as food banks, mental health resources, and public health coverage for children. Provide accurate information about resources and make appropriate referrals to families in need. After making a referral, follow up with families to ensure children's needs are being met.

Primary-aged children are making health and safety decisions for themselves. Examples include wearing a helmet when riding a bicycle, brushing teeth, washing hands after using the restroom, making appropriate nutrition choices, and not talking to strangers. They are eager to gain competence and are receptive to learning about health concepts. Education is a powerful tool in helping children understand and implement health and safety concepts. Integrate basic health and safety concepts into your daily curriculum. Actively teach procedures for preventing the spread of infectious disease (see Appendix A) and prevention of substance abuse.

Preventing Substance Abuse

Not all substance abuse programs are effective—(some programs may even do more harm than good. Substance Abuse and Mental Health Service Administration (SAMHSA) Center for Drug Abuse Prevention Web site (see "Recommended Web Sites Section") provides research-based tools to help early childhood professionals develop prevention programs.

The National Institute on Drug Abuse (NIDA, 2006) states that prevention programs should focus on reducing risk factors (deviant attitudes, aggression, poor self-control) and building protective factors (parental support, personal interests). For younger children, risk factors inside the family are more likely than peers to contribute to substance abuse.

Early intervention prevents risk factors from developing and provides protective factors (emotional awareness, positive peer relationships, correct information). The NIDA recommends that elementary school prevention programs focus on building self-control, emotional awareness, communication, and social problem-solving skills, and offering needed academic supports, especially in reading.

MOTOR DEVELOPMENT

Children ages six through eight are full of energy and enthusiasm. Growing cognitive and motor abilities make it possible for primary-aged children to remember and apply rules during organized games and combine a variety of motor skills (see Table 1–37). Children enjoy testing these new abilities with peers, thus enhancing social opportunities. Regular physical activity (including recess breaks) also helps children process information and work more efficiently in the classroom, and it serves as an outlet for helping children cope with stress. Fine motor skills improve, and through writing and drawing children express emotions and thoughts, communicate with others, and deepen their understanding of language (Charlesworth, 2008; see motor and language development discussions in "Children Ages Three Through Six" section).

Your Role: Motor Development

At times it may be difficult to balance the demands of academic standards and children's need for activity. It is not uncommon for first- and second-grade classrooms to concentrate more on reading and math instruction and provide fewer opportunities to practice gross and fine motor skills. Skillful time management is a key factor in providing opportunities for physical activity.

Your role in supporting motor development includes structuring your schedule to provide ample time for both gross and fine motor activity. Throughout the primary grades, children need to use manipulatives, sensory materials (clay, sand, and water), and writing, drawing, and art materials to further develop fine motor skills. You can encourage these skills by setting up your classroom to include activities such as journaling, art centers, puzzles, games, and construction materials (e.g., Legos, blocks, k-nex) and planning time for self-directed activities when fine motor skills can be practiced (see motor and language development discussions in "Children Ages Three Through Six" section).

The National Association for Sport and Physical Education (NASPE, 2006) reports that recess has significant physical, social, and cognitive benefits and is a critical aspect of supporting well-balanced development. During recess, children can explore movement, participate in physical activities, and work cooperatively with others. Physical activity also helps prevent health problems, including obesity (see physical growth discussion in "Children

TABLE 1–37   MOTOR DEVELOPMENT CHARACTERISTICS OF CHILDREN AGES SIX THROUGH EIGHT

Child's Name _____   Date _____

Motor Development	Date
6 years old	
Gross motor	
Muscle strength is increasing, boys usually stronger than girls	
Large and fine motor skills are refining; move with greater precision and deliberateness	
Likes physical activity: running, jumping, climbing, and throwing	
Moves constantly, even when trying to sit still	
Eye-hand coordination and complex motor skills are developing—riding a bicycle, swimming, swinging a bat, and kicking a ball	
Fine motor	
Writes letters and numbers with varying degrees of precision and interest; may reverse or confuse some letters: b/p, d/b, p/q, f/t	
Ties own shoes (some children may struggle)	
Folds and cuts paper into simple shapes	
Traces around hand and other objects	
Enjoys art projects: likes to paint, model with clay, "make things," draw and color, work with wood	
7 years old	
Gross motor	
Large and fine motor control is more finely tuned: runs up and down stairs alternating feet, throws and catches smaller balls, balances on either foot	
May be cautious when trying challenging physical activities, such as climbing up or jumping down from high places	
Practices a new motor skill repeatedly until mastered then moves on to something else	
Finds floor more comfortable than furniture when reading or watching television; legs often in constant motion	
Fine motor	
Is confident and deliberate in writing letters and numbers; characters are becoming more uniform; may run out of room at the end of a line or end of the page when writing	
Uses knife and fork appropriately, but inconsistently	
Tightly grasps pencil near the tip; rests head on forearm, lowers head almost to the tabletop when doing pencil-and-paper tasks	

(Continued)

TABLE 1–37   MOTOR DEVELOPMENT CHARACTERISTICS OF CHILDREN AGES SIX THROUGH EIGHT (*Continued*)

Motor Development	Date
8 years old	
Gross motor	
Likes physical activity—dancing, wrestling, bicycle, etc.	
Wants to participate in team activities and games: soccer, baseball, kickball	
Seems to have an endless supply of energy	
Significant gains in agility, balance, speed, and strength	
Fine motor	
Copies words and numbers from blackboard with increasing speed and accuracy; good eye-hand coordination	

Source: Adapted from *Developmental Profiles, Pre-Birth through Twelve* (5th ed.), by K. D. Allen & L. R. Marotz, 2007, Clifton Park, NY: Thomson Delmar Learning. Reprinted with permission of Delmar Learning, a division of Thomson Learning: http://www.thomsonrights.com. Fax 800 730-2215.

Aged Three Through Six" section). Other guidelines provided for teachers from the NASPE include the following:

- Schedule at least 60 minutes of physical activity and recess each day.

- Provide both structured activities with moderate to high physical intensity and unstructured activities.

- Value physical activity and recess as important parts of healthy development and education, and avoid using recess or physical activity to punish or reward children.

- Teach social skills during recess and physical education, and set firm limits that discourage aggressive behavior.

- Use only equipment and playground facilities that are safe and developmentally appropriate.

Young (1997) recommends that physical education should emphasize the health-related concepts and motor skills needed for a lifetime of physical health. Curriculum should focus on the following goals (Young, 1997, p. 4).

- mastery of basic skills

- application of cognitive concepts about physical activity and motor skills

- helping children to appreciate social diversity through social and cooperative skills

- the use of assessment methods that increase understanding and improve fitness of children

COGNITIVE DEVELOPMENT

During the primary grades, cognitive development expands rapidly. Logical thinking abilities are changing as children transition from preschool to kindergarten and on to first grade. However, children continue to learn through active exploration. The NAEYC (1995) specifies that the role of developmentally appropriate classrooms is to focus on creating smooth transitions for children by attending to individual needs and ensuring that development is moving forward, rather than limiting the progress of children with standardized readiness tests. In order to construct developmentally appropriate curriculum for children ages six through eight, cognitive abilities must be considered.

Throughout the primary grades children are becoming accustomed to newfound logical thinking abilities. They are increasingly able to take the perspective of others, mentally reverse actions, and focus on more than one aspect of a problem. These skills are needed for children to recognize that changing the shape of a ball of clay or pouring water into a different-shaped container does not change the original amount of material. This recognization means children can successfully conserve volume. As children gain the ability to conserve, mathematical abilities increase and control over mental processes such as memory and evaluation improve (Piaget & Inhelder, 1969; see Table 1–38). Children use these abilities as they carefully make plans and consciously implement strategies, such as mentally repeating things to increase memory. Advances in cognitive abilities also lead to self-awareness of thoughts and actions, resulting in self-evaluation. Additionally, children become aware that there are correct and incorrect responses to some learning tasks and may feel self-conscious about getting the wrong answer. Curriculum should be thoughtfully structured to help children avoid fear of failure and develop intrinsic motivation (Bodrova & Leong, 1996). Keep in mind that throughout the primary grades, children's learning needs are transitioning,

TABLE 1–38   COGNITIVE DEVELOPMENT CHARACTERISTICS OF CHILDREN AGES SIX THROUGH EIGHT

Child's Name_____   Birth Date _____

Cognitive Development	Date
6 years old	
Shows increased attention; persists at tasks for longer periods, but effort is not always consistent	
Understands simple time elements such as *today, tomorrow, yesterday*, and concepts of motion (cars go faster than bicycles)	
Recognizes seasons and major holidays and the activities associated with each	
Enjoys puzzles, counting and sorting activities, paper-and-pencil mazes, and games that involve matching letters and words with pictures	
Identifies coins (pennies, nickel, dimes, and quarters)	
7 years old	
Understands concepts of space and time in both logical and practical ways: a year is "a long time"; 100 miles is "far away"	
Begins to grasp Piaget's concept of conservation (the shape of a container does not necessarily reflect what it can hold)	
Gains a better understanding of cause and effect: "If I'm late for school again, I'll be in big trouble"	
Shows an interest in counting and saving money	
Tells time by the clock and understands calendar time—days, months, years, seasons	
Plans ahead: "I'm saving this cookie for tonight"	
Is fascinated with magic tricks; wants to put on "shows" for parents and friends	
8 years old	
Collects, organizes, and displays items; bargains or trades with friends to obtain additional objects	
Can add and subtract multiple-digit numbers; learning multiplication	
Saves money and develops plans to earn cash; enjoys looking at catalogs and magazines for items to purchase	
Begins taking an interest in what others think and do; understands there are differences of opinion, cultures, distant countries	
Accepts challenge and responsibility with enthusiasm; delights in being asked to perform tasks at home and in school; interested in being rewarded	
Uses logic to understand and solve everyday problems; is systematic when looking for a misplaced toy	

TABLE 1–38 COGNITIVE DEVELOPMENT CHARACTERISTICS OF CHILDREN AGES SIX THROUGH EIGHT (*Continued*)	
Cognitive Development	**Date**
8 years old	
Likes to read and work independently; spends considerable time planning and making lists	
Understands perspective (shadow, distance, shape); drawings reflect more realistic portrayal of objects	

Source: Adapted from *Developmental Profiles, Pre-Birth through Twelve* (5th ed.), by K. D. Allen & L. R. Marotz, 2007, Clifton Park, NY: Thomson Delmar Learning. Reprinted with permission of Delmar Learning, a division of Thomson Learning: http://www.thomsonrights.com. Fax 800 730-2215.

but remain closely related to preschool children's. In order to help children remain motivated about learning, classroom design and curriculum should continue to provide active, hands-on learning experiences.

Your Role: Cognitive Development

As children move from kindergarten to first grade, their lives change quickly. School takes up a greater portion of the day and learning often becomes more formalized. However, development is continuous. Such abrupt changes in expectations are stressful for children. Children are developing feelings of intellectual competence and need to feel successful, while receiving accurate feedback and encouragement. Your role is to provide adult-guided activities that focus on specific content, are enriching, and generate accurate feedback to children. Primary-aged children do not really understand letter grades, and large-group, worksheet-type instruction can be stressful and create misconceptions (Charlesworth, 2008). Providing open-ended tasks that emphasize the process rather than the product and giving children individual feedback and encouragement will facilitate feelings of competence. The following section includes a few ideas to consider when planning DAP curriculum for children ages six through eight.

Curriculum

Children ages six through eight are active and learn through activity. The ability to solve problems is a crucial life skill, and children need real experiences to learn how to solve real problems. Buschman (2002) found that mathematic and science problem-solving skills develop in stages and through practice. Children begin needing concrete objects to try possible solutions with. They move on to using fingers to solve math problems, imitating others, and trial-and-error methods. They tend to repeat particular strategies, even if they don't work. With experience, they learn what does work and are able to apply previous experiences to new problems. Eventually, children develop innovative solutions and can describe how they solved the problem. This process requires practice with a variety of problems in different contexts. Child-initiated, active, engaging curriculum experiences facilitate this process. The self-checklist in Table 1–39 includes considerations for constructing appropriate curriculum.

LANGUAGE DEVELOPMENT

One of the most exciting aspects of teaching is watching children discover reading. Reading skills emerge as infants and toddlers mimic the actions of adults. Preschoolers may look at books and describe what they think the story may be (see Table 1–40 on p. 116). With experience, children become aware that print is associated with spoken words, and they look at the printed words while repeating text they have memorized. Learning to read is empowering to young children and increases their feelings of competence. They also enjoy reading along with peers and talking about what they are reading (Schickedanz, 1999). By first grade, children vary greatly in reading skills. Some children read independently, whereas others are just beginning. Beach (1996) identified appropriate skills children should acquire by first grade: The knowing basic literary vocabulary (*word, letter, sound,* etc.), understanding that words are made of sounds (phonemic awareness), and recognizing some words by sight. By second grade children become familiar with spelling patterns and begin to read more independently (Beach, 1996). McGee and Richgel (2004) identified basic skills necessary to master reading. These skills include:

- comprehension of stories and informational texts

- being able to learn the meaning of new words

- using sound–letter relationships to decode new words

- the ability to spell words and use writing for different purposes

TABLE 1–39 PLANNING APPROPRIATE CURRICULUM SELF-CHECKLIST

	Rarely	Sometimes	Frequently
Curriculum decisions are based on knowledge of child development and the needs of children.			
Play is used as a vehicle for learning.			
Children are involved in planning and evaluating learning. They may choose from a menu of activities.			
Sense of community is emphasized by arrangement of furniture (tables rather than desks) and through collaborative projects.			
Curriculum is structured using learning centers and self-directed activities. Time limits and regimented sequences are avoided.			
Learning across developmental domains is integrated through structured investigations or projects based on the interests of children.			
Directed types of learning are introduced age appropriately.			
Games with rules are used to promote learning and self-regulation.			
Workbooks or worksheet instruction is avoided.			
Large-group or direct instruction for more than 20 to 30 minutes is avoided.			
Small-group and cooperative learning strategies are used as children are taught to compare, hypothesize, question, evaluate, and use negotiation skills.			
Children actively study topics of interest by planning, researching, experimenting, and presenting findings.			
Letter grades are avoided.			
Specific feedback based on effort and improvement is given.			
Children and families are involved in assessments, planning, and choosing adaptations for special needs.			
Family goals are identified and pursued, and families are educated about DAP and its implications for children.			
Identify one goal for personal improvement and reevaluate your progress in two weeks. Goal:			

Source: Adapted from *Understanding Child Development* (7th ed.), by R. Charlesworth, 2008, Clifton Park, New York: Thomson Delmar Learning; and "My Transition from Conventional to More Developmentally Appropriate Practices in the Primary Grades," by J. Pelander, 1997, *Young Children, 52*(7), 19–25.

TABLE 1–40   LANGUAGE DEVELOPMENT CHARACTERISTICS OF CHILDREN AGES SIX THROUGH EIGHT

Child's Name_____   Birth Date _____

Language Development	Date
6 years old	
Loves to talk, often nonstop; may be described as a chatterbox	
Carries on adult-like conversations; asks many questions	
Learns 5 to 10 new words daily; vocabulary consists of 10,000 to 14,000 words	
Uses appropriate verb tenses, word order, and sentence structure	
Uses language (not tantrums or physical aggression) to express displeasure: "That's mine! Give it back, you dummy"	
Talks self through steps required in simple problem-solving situations (although the "logic" may be unclear to adults)	
Enjoys being read to and making up stories	
Writes letters and numbers and may confuse or reverse some letters and numbers: b/d, 6/9	
7 years old	
Likes to read and being read to	
Enjoys storytelling; likes to write short stories; tells imaginative tales	
Uses adult-like sentence structure and language in conversation; speech reflects cultural and geographical differences	
Use of language is more precise and elaborate; more descriptive adjectives and adverbs are used	
Uses gestures to illustrate conversations	
Criticizes own performance: "I didn't draw that right," "Her picture is better than mine"	
Verbal exaggeration is commonplace: "I ate 10 hot dogs at the picnic"	
Describes personal experiences in great detail	
Reading is becoming easier; may read for enjoyment	
Reading skills tend to be ahead of spelling skills	
May still reverse letters or substitute some sounds	
8 years old	
Delights in telling jokes and riddles	
Understands and carries out multiple-step instructions (up to five steps); may need directions repeated because of not listening to the entire request	
Enjoys writing letters or sending e-mail messages to friends; includes imaginative and detailed descriptions	

TABLE 1–40   LANGUAGE DEVELOPMENT CHARACTERISTICS OF CHILDREN AGES SIX THROUGH EIGHT (*Continued*)

Language Development	Date
8 years old	
Uses language to criticize or compliment others; repeats slang and curse words	
Understands and follows rules of grammar in conversation and written form	
Is intrigued with learning secret word codes and using code language	
Converses fluently with adults; can think and talk about past and future: "What time are we leaving to get to the swim meet next week?"	
Reads with ease and understanding	
Writes notes or sends e-mails to friends that are imaginative and detailed	

Source: Adapted from *Developmental Profiles, Pre-Birth through Twelve* (5th ed.), by K. D. Allen & L. R. Marotz, 2007, Clifton Park, NY: Thomson Delmar Learning. Reprinted with permission of Delmar Learning, a division of Thomson Learning: http://www.thomsonrights.com. Fax 800 730-2215.

Writing develops from speech and drawing. Written expression demonstrates children's ability to use symbols and language. Social interactions with adults and peers facilitate this process as children discuss and evaluate their writing. Open-ended writing is more motivating for children. In open-ended writing opportunities, children's writing usually repeats themes they build on over time (Charlesworth, 2008).

Your Role: Supporting Language Skills

Enjoyment of reading and writing is perhaps as important as developing the basic skills. Your role is to facilitate enjoyment of and competency in literacy skills through meaningful activities based on the interests and needs of children. Children need ample time to explore and practice reading and writing in a relaxed environment—around 50 percent of class time (Allington, 2002). Primary-aged children enjoy projects and working toward a goal with peers. Be creative and integrate reading and writing activities into other areas. For example, use dramatic play for writing scripts and performing written material, art for illustrations of stories and poems, or have children write notes to communicate with one another. Other suggestions from Allington (2002) and Beach (1996) for facilitating reading and writing during the primary years include the following (for more information, see language development discussion in "Children Ages Three Through Six" section):

- Use open-ended daily writing activities such as journals to encourage children to practice writing, connect real events with written language, and express creativity. Directly teach children cognitive strategies and model effecting reading strategies during authentic reading activities that have a purpose (avoid reading worksheets).

- Provide a wide variety of books on diverse topics, and books at a variety of reading levels (informational, picture, fairy tales, poetry, etc.).

- Ask children open-ended questions and encourage children to ask questions. Talk about and evaluate what they are reading and writing. "What would happen if . . .?", "What do you think will happen next?", "What would you have done?", "How else could the author have ended the story?", "What sound does [a word] start with?"

- Use progressive, meaningful writing assignments that take several days to complete, are based on personal experiences, are integrated with other areas of learning, and allow children to make choices. Examples include having children write a play, song, or poem about things they are interested in (often characters from the media).

- Read aloud to children daily (see Table 1–41 for recommended books). If you are reading a chapter book to older children, create a display of images or information pertaining to the book you are reading—for example: maps, pictures, charts, and timelines. Children can also help make the displays and document their learning.

- Integrate objects or food from stories into the curriculum to give children firsthand experience.

- Provide time and comfortable places for children to read to each other and share reading strategies with one another.

- Create language puzzles for children by writing messages and directions for children on chart paper, white board, or chalk board. Leave out words or letters and have the children predict what is missing and share the strategies they used to make their predictions. With experience, children can experiment with writing messages like this for others.

TABLE 1–41   RECOMMENDED BOOKS FOR KINDERGARTEN AND THE PRIMARY GRADES
Beginning Readers
Hoban: *Arthur's Back to School*
Lobel: *Frog and Toad Are Friends*
Mayer: *Nightmare in My Closet*
Parish: *Amelia Bedelia*
Rylant: *Henry and Fudge: Annie's Good Move*
Sharmat: *Nate the Great*
Wardlaw: *Hector's Hiccups*
Chapter Books
Brown: *Arthur* series
Danziger: *Amber Brown* series
DePaola: *26 Fairmont Avenue*
Kline: *The Horrible Harry* series
Park: *Junie B. Jones* series
Christopher: *Man Out at First; The Kid Who Only Hits Homers*
Osborne: *The Magic Treehouse* series; *Blizzard of the Blue Moon; Night of the New Magicians*
Byars: *Tornado; Midnight Fox; Not-Just-Anybody Family; Wanted . . . Mud Blossom; Black Towers*

SOCIAL-EMOTIONAL DEVELOPMENT

During the primary years, peer relationships take center stage. Social and moral understandings are constructed as children navigate real-life dilemmas. Peer relationships have the ability to meet many of children's social and emotional needs by providing companions to practice the give and take of relationships and cooperative decision making. To develop friendships, children need to be able to approach others appropriately, play cooperatively, engage in conversations, and accept more than one solution to problems. Children that struggle socially usually don't understand that their negative behaviors are ineffective. They may be puzzled at the negative responses they receive and blame others. Behaviors such as aggression, disruptiveness, and shyness may either lead to rejection of a peer or be a result of being rejected. Rejection from peers usually results in feelings of loneliness. Rejected children and children who reject peers benefit from being directly taught appropriate social skills in a sensitive manner during everyday situations (Hart, McGee, & Hernandez, 1993).

Primary-aged children are more aware of differences among people and begin comparing themselves to others. Primary-aged children recognize appropriate and inappropriate behaviors and want things to be "fair" (equal shares or treatment). All children need to learn about their own ethnic group and other ethnic groups to prevent misconceptions about differences, and to develop a healthy self-concept. Children need practice in resolving everyday social problems to develop moral reasoning skills (Damon, 1988). Successfully resolving real problems and accomplishing tasks creates feelings of self-esteem. Cooperative learning strategies naturally motivate primary-aged children by providing opportunities to build competencies and complete tasks with peers (Charlesworth, 2008). (See Table 1–42.)

Your Role: Supporting Social-Emotional Development

Warm, supportive relationships continue to provide the foundation for social-emotional development. Children ages six through eight are striving to feel competent and productive. As language abilities increase they express greater self-understanding. Most children enjoy sharing thoughts and feelings, especially with peers. They frequently ask questions in order to understand decision-making processes. Teaching through conversations about everyday issues helps them to apply decision-making skills to life situations. Your role is to facilitate meaningful classroom relationships and social problem solving.

Class meetings are a tool some teachers use to help children practice democratic problem solving, build a sense of community, and foster self-esteem. Class meetings are times when the class meets together in a common area of the room to discuss concerns impacting the group. Topics of meetings may include: schedule changes, planning, study topics, and resolving group problems. The teacher's role is that of a facilitator, guiding children to clearly identify the problem and desired outcome. Children brainstorm and negotiate appropriate solutions. Your role is to allow children to try solutions (if no danger is involved) even if they may not work. Children learn through making choices and experiencing results (National Education Association, 2006). (For more information, visit http://www.nea.org/classmanagement.) The self-evaluation in Table 1–43 (see p. 123) covers teaching practices that help children develop peer relationships. The following information provides strategies for facilitating the development of self-concept.

TABLE 1–42　SOCIAL-EMOTIONAL DEVELOPMENT CHARACTERISTICS OF CHILDREN AGES SIX THROUGH EIGHT

Name_____　　　　Birth Date _____

Social-Emotional Development	Date
6 years old	
Experiences mood swings—loving then uncooperative and irritable, especially toward mother or primary caregiver	
Becomes less dependent on parents as peer relationships expand; needs closeness and nurturing but wants independence	
Plays cooperatively with other children and completes cooperative projects	
Shows respect for and interest in adults (parents, teachers, etc.)	
Needs and seeks adult approval, reassurance, and praise; may complain excessively about minor hurts to gain more attention	
Takes turns when playing games with others	
Remains egocentric; sees events almost entirely from own perspective: everything and everyone is to benefit them	
7 years old	
Is cooperative and affectionate toward adults most of the time; sees humor in everyday happenings	
Likes to be the teacher's helper and seeks teacher's attention and approval in less obvious ways	
Seeks to build friendships; friends are important, but can entertain self	
Participates in play activities and projects with peers that require cooperation and rule observance	
Makes up own rules to games to increase chances of winning	
Likes opportunities to take responsibility and can carry out directions	
Quarrels less often, although squabbles and tattling continue in both one-on-one and group play	
Complains that family decisions are unjust—that a particular sibling gets to do more or is given more	
Blames others for own mistakes; makes up alibis for personal shortcomings: "I could have made a better one, but my teacher didn't give me enough time"	
8 years old	
Begins forming opinions about moral values and attitudes; declares things right or wrong	
Plays with two or three "best" friends, most often the same age and gender; also enjoys spending some time alone	

(Continued)

TABLE 1–42   SOCIAL-EMOTIONAL DEVELOPMENT CHARACTERISTICS OF CHILDREN AGES SIX THROUGH EIGHT (*Continued*)

Social-Emotional Development	Date
8 years old	
More accepting of own performance but easily frustrated when unable to complete a task or when the product does not meet expectations	
Continues to blame others or make up reasons for mistakes	
Desires adult attention and recognition; likes to perform for adults	
Enjoys talking on the telephone with friends	
Feels competent; is willing to practice skills until mastery is achieved and feels successful in one or more areas	
Describes likes and dislikes about self; has a generally moderate to high self-esteem and positive self-concept	

Source : Adapted from *Developmental Profiles, Pre-Birth through Twelve* (5th ed.), by K. D. Allen & L. P. Marotz, 2007, Clifton Park, NY: Thomson Delmar Learning. Reprinted with permission of Delmar Learning, a division of Thomson Learning: http://www.thomsonrights.com. Fax 800 730-2215.

Self-Concept

Primary-aged children notice differences in family income, behaviors, intelligence, values, culture, religion, and appearance. Families and children may feel self-conscious, or may feel that their values are threatened as primary-age children begin engaging with a broader group of peers. Children need guidance to promote flexibility in their thinking as they come to understand that there are many appropriate ways of thinking, behaving, and solving problems. Your relationship with children is the best tool for helping them develop these characteristics (Damon, 1988). The personal relationship you build with children is a powerful model. When children have a sense of security and self-worth it becomes easier to value, accept, and appreciate themselves—and others. Teaching human dignity, appreciation, cooperation, social problem solving, and acceptance is not a theme or unit. These concepts are imbedded in almost every interaction between teachers and children. Such integration requires that teachers consciously reflect on their own values and behaviors. Ideas for developing inclusion and diversity in the classroom include the following (see Table 1–44 on p. 124):

■ Make children's families and cultures part of the classroom. Create a bulletin board for pictures of families and encourage families to participate in classroom activities.

■ Choose picture books that introduce children to diverse cultures, with illustrations that represent diverse people.

TABLE 1–43   SUPPORTING SOCIAL DEVELOPMENT SELF-CHECKLIST

	B	P	M
I provide warm, relaxed, affectionate interactions with children.			
I spend time actively listening to children each day.			
I note children's strengths by giving positive feedback, encouraging them to help peers, and providing activities that help them build their talents.			
I model effective communication and social skills.			
I provide accurate and constructive feedback about children's efforts and abilities.			
I teach specific social skills to individual children, as needed, during daily interactions.			
I use cooperative games and activities as teaching strategies.			
I provide self-directed time for children, both indoors and on the playground.			
I hold class meetings to discuss issues affecting the entire class.			
I set firm expectations for prosocial behavior.			
I teach prosocial behavior and provide opportunities for children to practice prosocial behaviors.			
I provide opportunities for children to get to know one another and each other's families.			
I provide opportunities for children to explore similarities and appreciate differences.			
I use teaching and discussion strategies that encourage children to take the perspective of others.			
I emphasize the learning process and mastery of effective academic skills (persistence, problem solving, collaboration) rather than correct and incorrect answers.			

Directons: *Use this checklist to evaluate your skills in supporting the social development of primary-age children.*

Beginning (B): *You are aware of and understand the criteria.*

Progressing (P): *You are implementing and experimenting with the criteria.*

Mastery (M): *You understand how to adapt the criteria to fit the individual needs of children.*

Source: Adapted from *Guidance of Young Children* (6th ed.), by M. Marion, 2002, New York: Prentice Hall; and *Understanding Child Development* (7th ed.), by R. Charlesworth, 2008, Clifton Park, NY: Thomson Delmar Learning.

TABLE 1–44   SUPPORTING HEALTHY SELF-CONCEPT SELF-CHECKLIST

	Rarely	Sometimes	Frequently
I provide opportunities for children to learn while pursuing their own interests.			
I acknowledge and accept the feelings children experience.			
I set challenging, achievable goals with children and provide appropriate support through scaffolding.			
I encourage hard work, individual effort, and collaboration with others.			
I emphasize that mistakes are part of learning.			
I avoid having children compete and making comparisons between children.			
I provide opportunities for children to take on classroom responsibilities and make age-appropriate decisions.			
I respect the individual pacing and temperament of children.			
I value cultural, individual, and ethnic diversity in everyday ways (e.g., inviting all children to share their cultures, values, celebrations, and beliefs in the classroom; including family visitors, books, stories, songs, games, foods).			
I learn about the culture of children in my classroom.			
I am aware of and respect differences in communication style.			
I teach children about communication differences.			
I expose children to a variety of cultures in an authentic manner by inviting members of diverse cultures to participate in classroom activities and share their values, beliefs, and traditions.			
I avoid using gender or cultural stereotypes.			
I actively reflect upon my own beliefs and assumptions, seeking deeper understanding of others.			
Identify one goal for personal improvement and reevaluate your progress in two weeks. Goal:			

Source: Adapted from *Beyond Self-Esteem: Developing a Genuine Sense of Human Value*, by N. E. Curry & C. N. Johnson, 1991, Washington, DC: National Association for the Education of Young Children; and *Starting Small: Teaching Tolerance in Preschool and the Early Grades*, Teaching Tolerance, 1997. Montgomery, AL: Southern Poverty Law Center.

- Talk to children about differences in how people react to situations and the similarities people share (e.g., the common needs for love and belonging).

- Tactfully but honestly discuss difficulties in peer relationships with children. Help children recognize when behavior is harmful to their relationships with others.

- Connect academic concepts to real-life social problems. Provide opportunities for children to study "people," including anatomy, physiology, nutrition, personal hygiene, cultures, and religion. Learn what causes skin colors to vary (science). Read picture books about Martin Luther King Jr. or Ghandi. Hold a class meeting about equality and what respecting and valuing everyone means in your classroom.

Developmental Alerts

Children ages six through eight may have a variety of special needs ranging from motor disabilities to depression. The increasing focus on academics can lead to children with learning disabilities quickly falling behind. Early detection of special needs and appropriate intervention continue to be key aspects of supporting children's development. Children need to be evaluated by a health professional or child development specialist if

By the sixth birthday the child

- cannot walk up and down stairs with alternating feet.

- speaks in a voice that is consistently too loud, too soft, too high, or too low.

- has difficulty following simple directions in order: "Pick-up the papers then put on your back pack."

- fails to construct appropriate sentences using four to five words.

- is unable to cut on a line with scissors.

- cannot sit still for five to seven minutes while listening to a story.

- avoids making eye contact when spoken to (unless this is a cultural taboo).

- has difficulty playing well with other children.

- does not independently care for self by brushing teeth, washing hands and face.

By the seventh birthday, the child

- is not continuing to gain in height and weight; has difficulty with motor development, such as running, jumping, balancing.

- has little interest in reading and trying to copy letters or writing, especially own name.

- is unable to follow simple, multiple-step directions: "Complete your project, clean up the materials, and put your coat on."

- cannot complete simple tasks and follow through with directions: cleaning up materials, hanging up coat, or finishing a puzzle. (Note: All children forget. Task incompletion is not a problem unless a child repeatedly leaves tasks unfinished.)

- does not develop prosocial methods as alternatives to excessive use of inappropriate behaviors in order to get own way.

- continues to show anxiety-type behaviors associated with starting school: repeated grimacing or facial tics, eye twitching, grinding of teeth, regressive soiling or wetting, frequent stomachaches, refusing to go to school.

If by the eighth birthday, the child

- cannot attend to the task at hand; cannot sit quietly for longer periods.

- has difficulty following through on simple directions.

- complains excessively about stomachaches or headaches when getting ready for school.

- plays alone most of the time or withdraws consistently from contact with other children.

- has frequent or recurring nightmares or bad dreams.

- squints, rubs eyes excessively, or frequently asks to have things repeated.

- displays excessive crying, sleeping or eating disturbances, withdrawal, or frequent anxiety.

- does not assume responsibility for personal care (dressing, bathing, feeding self) most of the time.

- lacks improvement with motor skills.

Adapt from *Developmental Profiles, Pre-Birth Through Twelve* (5th ed.), by K. D. Allen & L. R. Marotz, 2007. Reprinted with permission of Delmar Learning, a division of Thomson Learning: http://www.thomsonrights.com. Fax 800 730-2215.

SUPPORTING FAMILIES OF CHILDREN AGES SIX THROUGH EIGHT

Parents should be actively involved in educating and protecting their children. As children begin school, families may become increasingly concerned with academic achievement and social adjustment. Yet, communication with parents becomes more challenging as many do not accompany children to school each day. Some teachers may only see a parent two times a year for parent-teacher conferences. Under these circumstances, small, simple actions that bridge school and home go a long way. Pelander (1997) recommends beginning the school year by asking parents to identify goals for their children. Notes home, homework, and newsletters are other common ways to communicate with parents (see "Supporting Diverse Families" section). Although the initial efforts you make to build positive relationships with children and families may seem time consuming, they will result in smoother classroom functioning, better learning outcomes, and saved time in the long run. Some teachers ask parents questions when conducting a home visit, at parent-teacher conferences, or when parents come and go each day, to learn about children (see Table 1–45). You might also use these questions to create a questionnaire that parents can fill out and you can keep on file. Avoid asking too many questions at one time. This can feel overwhelming to parents. Be sensitive to their needs and patient in establishing relationships.

RECOMMENDED READINGS

Dyson, A. H. (1998). *Writing superheroes: Contemporary childhood, popular culture, and classroom literacy.* Teachers College Press. Focuses on ways to promote writing by using children's out-of-school and popular-culture experiences.

TABLE 1–45   CHILDREN AGES SIX THROUGH EIGHT FAMILY QUESTIONNAIRE

What are your child's strengths?
Do you have any concerns about your child?
Does your child enjoy reading activities? Please explain.
Does your child show an interest in writing? How?
What types of art and music interest your child?
Is your child using numbers? How?
How do you discipline your child?
Does your child have friends? What are their ages?
Is your child able to cooperate with others?
Does your child assertively communicate needs?
Does your child have any health concerns?
What types of media (TV, computer, Internet, video games, music, etc.) does your child use?
How many hours per day does your child spend using media?
How does your child feel about school?
Has your child had any difficult emotional events recently (e.g., deaths, moving, etc.)

Gullo, D. (Ed.). (2006). *K today: Teaching and learning in the kindergarten year.* NAEYC. (ISBN 978-928896-39-5). A comprehensive review of current best practices, including investigation, assessment, development, and planning curriculum during the kindergarten year.

Owocki, G. (2001). *Make way for literacy: Teaching the way young children learn.* Heinemann & the NAEYC. (ISBN 0-325-00270-3). Provides practical curriculum ideas on supporting the development of literacy and building a sense of community.

Stone, J. (2001). *Building classroom community: The early childhood teacher's role.* NAEYC. (ISBN 0-935989-98-6). The teacher's role in leading and guiding the building of a community within the classroom is discussed and a model is presented. Other topics include creating a caring community environment, building respect, and helping children with difficult behavior in a way that maintains their sense of dignity.

RECOMMENDED WEB SITES

Center for Early Education and Development (CEED): http://education.umn.edu. Information about children (birth to age eight), includes special needs.

Center for Effective Collaboration and Practice (CECP): http://cecp.air.org. Helps communities create programs that promote emotional well-being and effective instruction.

National Association for Sports and Physical Education: http://www.aahperd.org. The NASPE is a nonprofit professional membership association. Its Web site provides position statements and resources about physical activity for children and youth.

National Institute on Drug Abuse: htttp://www.drugabuse.gov. This organization hosts a Web site that outlines principles in substance abuse prevention and provides research-based guidelines for instituting prevention programs. A guidebook for parents, educators, and communities can be downloaded. Provides a curriculum—"Brain Power: Junior Scientist"—for grades K–5.

PE Central: http://www.pecentral.org. Health and physical education resources, including lesson plans.

SAMHSA's Center for Drug Abuse Prevention: http://prevention.samhsa.gov/. Provides a science-based substance abuse prevention planning guide and resources for educators.

See also "Recommanded Web Sites" in "Children Ages Three Through Six" section.

SPECIAL NEEDS

Like other children in your classroom, no two children with special needs are alike. Children with special needs may have genetic disorders, birth defects, sensory/motor impairments, and/or emotional, social, behavioral, learning, or mental difficulties. These conditions are influenced by a variety of factors and can range from mild to severe in how they impact learning and development. It is not unusual for children to have more than one condition occur together (e.g., communication and behavior, or sensory and learning; Wolery & Wilbers, 1994). This section provides an overview of working with children with special needs.

Early identification of conditions that may impair development is critical. Young children may not be identified until they come in contact with an early childhood professional. Core knowledge of child development and the factors that influence development is your best tool for identifying delays. Concerns are typically identified through routine daily observations (see "Observation" and "Developmental Alerts" sections). Identification methods include observations, developmental screening scales, and sensory screening (Wolery & Wilbers, 1994). States differ in how specific identification and education services are administered. It is best to learn about the programs and services available in your state. Places and people that may provide screening for identification of special needs include the following:

- school districts and special education professionals
- state health and education departments
- hospitals and health care professionals
- Head Start, Even Start, and early intervention programs

- mental health centers and professionals

- speech and language professionals

If you have concerns, do not wait to see if the child will "grow out of it." Often, the child will not (Wolery & Wilbers, 1994). Discuss the situation in a sensitive manner with colleagues who are involved with the child and the child's family. Then make an appropriate referral and follow up to ensure services are appropriate and meet the needs of the child and family.

The Individuals with Disabilities Education Act (IDEA; P.L. 105–17) ensures educational assistance to young children with disabilities. This act stipulates that schools have the responsibility of including students with disabilities in general education classrooms. Early intervention programs serve children younger than school aged. Services for children younger than three are usually based on an individualized family service plan (IFSP). The IFSP outlines the services to be provided to infants and toddlers. It includes the abilities and needs of the child, resources and goals of the family, desired outcomes, and intervention services. After the age of three, intervention for children is outlined through an individual education program (IEP) developed by a team of experts who work with the child. This team usually includes parents, teachers, and professional specialists (Katz & Schery, 2006).

Participating in this process will probably be a new experience for you. You may find the special education jargon and acronyms unfamiliar and confusing. Don't hesitate to ask questions, and be patient with yourself. Learning special education terminology and procedures will help you meet the needs of children and grow as a professional. The most important information for you to understand is (Katz & Schery, 2006; Wolery & Wilbers, 1994)

- the child's capabilities and needed adaptations.

- how the child learns best, and how to help the child feel welcomed.

- resources and goals of the family, including strategies and methods to use.

You will also need to implement interventions, share information with the team, and support families in their goals for children.

Effective intervention greatly improves the learning and develop-ment of children with special needs. The other children in your class will also benefit. Playing and functioning with peers who have a variety of abilities helps children develop respect, empathy, and new ways of interacting (Villa & Colker, 2006). You can help children develop a sense of community and see the perspective of others by preparing children to welcome a peer with special needs. Here are a few suggestions to help children adjust (Katz & Schery, 2006):

- Use activities and books to help children become familiar with assistive devices and understand the special conditions. For example, allow children to investigate and try a wheelchair, or try to function while blind-folded, wearing ear muffs, or using only one arm.

- Role-play adaptations children may need to make to communicate with peers with special needs (e.g., speaking more slowly or using sign language).

- Teach children that everyone has abilities and challenges.

The manner in which special needs conditions affect children's learning and development is influenced by time of onset, how soon the disability was identified, and the availability of services to fam-ilies (Katz & Schery, 2006; Wolery & Wilbers, 1994). The future ability of children to progress developmentally across all domains is significantly dependent on how much their condition restricts their participation in classroom activities. Keep in mind that con-ditions requiring intervention will often change (sometimes even daily). It is important to continually observe, assess, and adapt practices accordingly (Katz & Schery, 2006). Your beliefs about dis-abilities will significantly impact how you implement interven-tions. Villa and Colker (2006, p. 97) note that effective practices are based on three beliefs.

- Every child can learn.

- Every child is unique.

- Every child is important.

The more independently children function in the classroom, the less disabilities will impact their overall development. Children who have special needs may require classroom adaptations in order to help them fully participate in activities. Assistive technology helps children participate in age-appropriate activities with peers, function as independently as possible, and communicate effectively.

High-tech assistive devices include computers or voice synthesizers, while low-tech devices include paintbrushes with special handles and stools for reaching things (Mulligan, 2003). Be creative. Thoughtfully plan your environment and teaching strategies according to the needs and learning abilities of all children in your class. Villa and Colker (2006) also note the following helpful strategies:

- Collaborate with a special education colleague for ideas and support.

- Plan time in your day to clearly communicate daily progress and goals with parents, other teachers, and assistants.

- Have appropriate expectations. Problems will occur. Take them day by day and actively seek solutions based on individual daily needs.

- Encourage children to help one another solve difficulties.

The following information includes a brief description of some of the common special needs that emerge during early childhood. As you work and learn with children with special needs and their families, you will have the opportunity to deepen your understanding of development and developmentally appropriate practices. Develop problem-solving skills and, most important, provide equal learning opportunities for all children.

ATTENTION DEFICIT HYPERACTIVITY DISORDER (ADHD)

ADHD has been referred to by several other names, including ADD (attention deficit disorder). Currently, three types of ADHD are recognized: hyperactive-impulsive, inattentive, and combined. Between 3 and 7 percent of school-aged children are affected by ADHD. Difficulty maintaining attention, impulsive behavior, and overactivity are key characteristics (National Institute of Mental Health [NIMH], 2006a).

Hyperactive-impulsive signs of ADHD include the following:

- fidgeting

- restlessness

- frequently leaving seat

- blurting out answers, or having trouble waiting for a turn

Inattentive signs of ADHD include the following:

- becoming distracted by irrelevant sights and sounds
- failing to attend to details
- careless mistakes
- difficulty following instructions
- frequently losing things
- leaving activities uncompleted

Many children will display some of these characteristics occasionally. To be diagnosed with ADHD, children must manifest the symptoms to a degree that is inappropriate for their age, for at least six months. Behavioral and pharmaceutical interventions are available to treat ADHD. Psychologists, psychiatrists, pediatricians, clinical social workers, and neurologists can diagnose ADHD (NIMH, 2006a).

AUTISM

The Center for Disease Control and Prevention (CDC, 2005) describes autism spectrum disorders (ASD) as a group of developmental disabilities identified by difficulty with social interaction, problems in communication, and unusual behaviors or interests. Children with ASD may have unconventional methods of learning, trouble staying on task, or problems with responding to stimulation. The onset of ASD occurs before the age of three. It is four times more likely to occur in boys than girls. The following are symptoms of ASD.

- may not like being held or cuddled
- may not notice when others talk to them
- may be interested in others but doesn't know how to interact with or relate to them
- may not talk at all
- may repeat back things they have heard or that are said to them
- may have difficulty taking turns in conversation
- may repeat actions over and over
- may have difficulty when routines change

Children with ASD may have average motor skills yet significant delays in language, social, and cognitive skills. They can struggle with making friends, yet have strong skills at putting puzzles together. They may be reading rather long words, but not be able to identify specific letter sounds. Children with ASD may learn a skill and then lose it. They may be saying many words, then stop talking. Children with ASD need the support of medical and mental health professionals (CDC, 2005).

DOWN SYNDROME

The National Dissemination Center for Children with Disabilities (NICHCY, 2004a) reports that there is a wide variation in mental abilities, behavior, and developmental progress in individuals with Down syndrome. Their level of retardation may range from mild to severe, with the majority functioning in the mild to moderate range. Due to these individual differences, it is impossible to predict future achievements of children with Down syndrome. Some of the common characteristics of children with Down syndrome include the following:

- poor muscle tone

- slanting eyes with folds of skin at the inner corners (called epicanthal folds)

- hyperflexibility (excessive ability to extend the joints)

- short, broad hands with a single crease across the palm on one or both hands

- flat bridge of the nose

- small head

Individuals with Down syndrome are usually smaller than their peers, and their physical and intellectual development is slower. Heart defects; gastrointestinal tract problems; visual, hearing, and speech and language problems; and obesity can also be issues. Developmental intervention provides special instruction for parents in teaching their child language, cognitive, self-help, and social skills, and specific exercises for gross and fine motor development. Continuing education, positive public attitudes, and a stimulating home environment have also been found to promote the child's overall development (NICHCY, 2004a). Implications for teachers include the following (NICHCY, 2004a):

- Emphasize concrete concepts rather than abstract ideas.

- Teach tasks in a step-by-step manner with frequent reinforcement and consistent feedback.

- Provide appropriate nutrition and opportunities for physical activity.

- Avoid limiting the child's capabilities.

ENGLISH LANGUAGE LEARNERS (ELLs)

You may have children in your classroom who are learning English. The primary language of a child may be a different dialect of English or a different language. Children who are learning English may have cognitive abilities ahead of there English verbal abilities. They need support that allows them to continue to participate and grow cognitively while their English language abilities are developing (McLaughlin, 1992). When learning a second language, children may be silent for a period when first exposed to a new language. They are listening and trying to comprehend. This may last as long as a year for preschoolers. As English acquisition begins, learners may construct sentences using words from both languages. The goals for children learning a second language should include maintaining and developing skills in their primary language (Roseberry-McKibbin & Brice, 1997–2006). Things to keep in mind when working with ELL students include the following:

- *Be patient:* It takes about two years for children to acquire basic social communication skills in a second language (Roseberry-McKibbin & Brice, 1997–2006). See things from their point of view. They may feel awkward due to a new context and environment (McLaughlin, 1992).

- *Keep teaching language:* Academic language skills may be behind social communication skills. A child may be able to converse, yet still need help mastering grammar and writing (McLaughlin, 1992; Roseberry-McKibbin & Brice, 1997–2006).

- *Integrate both languages in the classroom*: First-language skills are still developing and children need to develop skills in both languages (Browyn, 2003). Use of their primary (home) language while learning a second language is beneficial. Immerse them in language and encourage them to make connections between their primary language and English (McLaughlin, 1992; National Center for Research on Cultural Diversity and Second Language Learning [NCRDSLL], 1995). Enrich your classroom by allowing ELL learners to share their culture and primary language with peers (Browyn, 2003).

■ *Individualize:* Not all children learn language in the same way. Individual learning styles and preferences affect how children will best learn a language (McLaughlin, 1992; NCRDSLL, 1995)

EMOTIONAL/BEHAVIORAL DISORDERS

The NIMH (2006b) reports that many everyday stresses can cause changes in behavior. The birth of a sibling may cause a child to temporarily act much younger. It is important to recognize such behavior changes, but also to differentiate them from signs of more serious problems. Problems deserve attention when they

■ are severe.

■ are persistent.

■ impact daily activities.

Seek help for children if you observe the following problems.

■ changes in appetite or sleep

■ social withdrawal

■ fearfulness

■ behavior that seems to slip back to an earlier phase, such as bed-wetting

■ signs of distress such as sadness or tearfulness

■ self-destructive behavior such as head banging

■ tendency to have frequent injuries

If you observe these behaviors, document them and include the frequency, intensity, and duration. In addition, review the overall development of the child, considering any important medical problem he or she might have had, family history of mental disorders, and physical and psychological traumas or situations that may cause stress. Professionals who can help children with these issues include doctors, psychiatrists, psychologists, social workers, and behavioral therapists (NIMH, 2006b).

LEARNING DISABILITIES (LD)

The National Dissemination Center for Children with Disabilities ([NICHCY], 2004b) explains that there is no single sign that shows a person has a learning disability. Experts look for a noticeable difference between how well a child does in school and how well he or she *could* do, given his or her intelligence or ability. There are also certain clues that may mean a child has a learning disability. Most relate to elementary school tasks, because learning disabilities tend to be identified in elementary school. A child probably will not show all of these signs, or even most of them. However, if a child shows a number of these problems, then parents and the teacher should consider the possibility that the child has a learning disability. When a child has a learning disability, he or she

- may have trouble learning the alphabet, rhyming words, or connecting letters to their sounds.

- may make many mistakes when reading aloud, and repeat and pause often.

- may not understand what he or she reads.

- may have real trouble with spelling.

- may have very messy handwriting or hold a pencil awkwardly.

- may struggle to express ideas in writing.

- may learn language late and have a limited vocabulary.

- may have trouble remembering the sounds that letters make or hearing slight differences between words.

- may have trouble understanding jokes, comic strips, and sarcasm.

- may have trouble following directions.

- may mispronounce words or use a wrong word that sounds similar.

- may have trouble organizing what he or she wants to say or not be able to think of the word he or she needs for writing or conversation.

- may not follow the social rules of conversation, such as taking turns, and may stand too close to the listener.

- may confuse math symbols and misread numbers.

- may not be able to retell a story in order (what happened first, second, third).

- may not know where to begin a task or how to go on from there.

If a child has unexpected problems learning to read, write, listen, speak, or do math, then teachers and parents may want to investigate more. The same is true if the child is struggling to do any one of these skills. The child may need to be evaluated to see if he or she has a learning disability. Teachers can help children with learning disabilities by

- breaking tasks into smaller steps, and giving directions verbally and in writing.

- giving the student more time to finish schoolwork or take tests.

- letting the student with reading problems use textbooks-on-tape (available through Recordings for the Blind and Dyslexic, listed in "Organizations" section).

- letting the student with listening difficulties borrow notes from a classmate or use a tape recorder.

- letting the student with writing difficulties use a computer with specialized software that spell checks, grammar checks, or recognizes speech.

- making test modifications to help a student with LD show what he or she has learned.

- teaching organizational skills, study skills, and learning strategies. These help all students but are particularly helpful to those with LD.

- working with the student's parents to create an educational plan tailored to meet the student's needs.

- establishing a positive working relationship with the student's parents. Through regular communication, exchange information about the student's progress at school (NICHCY, 2004b).

GIFTEDNESS

The National Association for Gifted Children (2005, p. 1) defines giftedness as "someone who shows, or has the potential for showing, an exceptional level of performance in one or more areas of expression." Indicators of giftedness in young children include:

- advanced vocabulary

- astute observations and curiosity

- deep understanding of complex concepts

- advanced critical thinking skills

- early indications of talents in the arts or athletics

Some difficulties gifted children may experience include the following (Webb, 1994, p. 2):

- *Uneven development.* For instance, fine motor skills may be behind cognitive development, resulting in frustration as children visualize what they want to accomplish but are unable to achieve.

- *Peer relations.* As preschoolers and in primary grades, gifted children (particularly highly gifted) attempt to organize people and things. This tendency to direct others may lead to resentment from others.

- *Perfectionism.* The ability to visualize ideals may lead them to the development of unrealistic expectations.

- *Avoidance of risk-taking.* The ability to visualize and predict possibilities may lead them to see potential problems in undertaking those activities.

- *Multipotentiality.* Gifted children often have several advanced capabilities and try to do too much.

Teachers can help gifted children by providing challenging but achievable curriculum, involving parents, and seeking parents' help in determining how the child learns best. Teachers should consider a variety of methods for meeting children's needs (Webb, 1994).

SHYNESS

Malouff (2002–2004) reports that shy behaviors are due to anxiety surrounding social situations and behavioral inhibitions. Shy children usually want to interact with others. Malouff suggests that teachers should support shy children by

- expressing empathy and sharing a personal example of feeling shy.

- pointing out the positive aspects of interacting with others.

- giving children plenty of time to respond to questions.

- modeling approachable behaviors.

- avoiding calling children "shy" and encouraging outgoing children to play with shy children.

Behavioral inhibition is a more severe, constant type of shyness. Children with behavioral inhibition usually have differences in temperament and cortisol levels compared with children who don't have this condition. They have difficulty adapting to social situations, are overvigilant and hesitant, and tend to react intensely to new experiences. It is important that these children receive professional treatment (NIMH, 2006c).

SPEECH AND LANGUAGE

Speech, language, and communication difficulties occur when language competencies lag behind age expectations. The NICHCY (2004c) describes delays and disorders as ranging from simple sound substitutions to the inability to understand or use language or use the oral-motor mechanism for functional speech and feeding. Characteristics of language disorders include the following:

- improper use of words and their meanings

- inability to express ideas

- inappropriate grammatical patterns

- reduced vocabulary and inability to follow directions

One or a combination of these characteristics may occur in children who are affected by language learning disabilities or developmental language delay. Children may hear or see a word but not be able to understand its meaning. They may have trouble getting others to understand what they are trying to communicate. Because all communication disorders carry the potential to isolate individuals from their social and educational surroundings, it is essential to find appropriate, timely intervention. Children with a language and speech disorder will usually work with a speech-language pathologist who will provide intervention strategies to parents and teachers.

RECOMMENDED READING

Chandler, P. A. (1994). *A place for me: including children with special needs in early care and education settings.* NAEYC. (ISBN 0935989595).

Gould, P., & Sullivan, J. (1999). *The inclusive early childhood classroom: Easy ways to adapt learning centers for all children.* Gryphon House. (ISBN 0876592035V).

Heidemann, S., & Hewitt, D. (1992). *Pathways to play: Developing play skills in young children.* Redleaf Press. (ISBN 0934140650). Critical social skills for engaging in cooperative play are identified and strategies for fostering children's development are included. Assessment and planning forms are provided.

McCracken, J. B. (Ed). (1985). *Reducing stress in the lives of young children.* NAEYC. (ISBN 0-935989-03-X). This is a collection of strategies from numerous professionals. Contents include coping with issues such as death, separation, hospitalization, and crisis. A section on strengthening families and avoiding stress in the classroom is also included.

Pfiffner, L. J. (1999). *All about ADHD: The complete practical guide for classroom teachers.* Scholastic Trade. (ISBN 0590251082). Scholastic. The goal of this book is to help teachers prepare for students with ADHD. A method for teaching students with ADHD that uses strategies for increasing learner readiness and behavior management is presented. Behavior problems and positive parent-teacher relationships are also addressed.

Rice, K. F., & Groves, B. M. (2005). *Hope & healing: A caregiver's guide to helping young children affected by trauma.* Zero to Three. (ISBN 0943657938).

Rief, S. F. (2005). *How to reach and teach ADD/ADHD children: Practical techniques, strategies, and interventions.* Jossey-Bass. (ISBN 0787972959).

Wolery, M., & Wilbers, J. (1994). *Including children with special needs in early childhood programs.* NAEYC. (ISBN 0-935989-61-7).

RECOMMENDED WEB SITES

Center for Applied Research in Education: http://www.btlocdes.org. Strategies for teaching students with ADHD. Includes organization, language arts, math, written language, study skills, classroom management, discipline, and relationships with parents. Covers elementary through high school age groups.

Children and Adults with Attention Deficit/Hyperactivity Disorder (CHADD): http://www.chadd.org. CHADD is a grass-roots organization that provides resources and encouragement for individuals with ADHD and parents, professionals, and educators. Includes listings for local chapters and professionals.

Council for Exceptional Children: http://www.cec.sped.org. This organization provides information to support professionals working with children with disabilities, exceptionalities, and giftedness. An excellent source for gaining greater insight into the special needs of children.

Learning Disabilities Association of America: http://www.ldanatl.org. This organization provides a fact sheet with excellent tips for involving parents in the assessment process.

National Association for Gifted Children (NAGC): http://www.nagc.org. This organization provides information for parents and educators on giftedness. Includes information on assessment, educational programs, what parents can do, and links to other sites.

National Association of School Psychologists: http://www.nasponline.org. This Web site provides a position statement from the organization on assessment in early childhood and the role of school psychologists. Includes recommended guidelines for assessment methods.

National Dissemination Center for Children with Disabilities: http//www.nichcy.org. Provides links, descriptions, and recommendations for a variety of disabilities.

National Institute of Mental Health (NIMH): http://www.nimh. nih.gov. NIMH provides information and research on mental and behavioral disorders.

National Resource Center on ADHD (NCR): http:// www.help4adhd.org. The NCR is a program of CHADD in cooperation with the Center for Disease Control and Prevention. This Web site provides information on diagnosis, living with ADHD, and education issues.

Tots 'n' Tech Research Institute: http://tnt.asu.edu. Provides information about assistive technology in children's lives. Great resource for teachers.

SUPPORTING DIVERSE FAMILIES

Children develop within the context of families, and each family has different values, experiences, and perceptions about raising children. Families also differ in terms of structure, interaction patterns, socioeconomic status, education, and culture. You will have the opportunity to support a variety of families in the task of raising well-adjusted children. When early childhood programs acknowledge the importance of families, practices become family centered. In family-centered programs teachers and families work together to create an atmosphere for children that is conducive to learning and healthy development, both at home and at school. Family-centered programs design services according to the needs of families and are based on three values (McBride, 1999, p. 62).

- Families are important for healthy development.

- Families are important decision makers in the lives of children.

- The role of early childhood professionals is to support families in raising children.

The program you work with may serve children from a wide variety of cultures. This is a wonderful opportunity for you to develop your knowledge about how culture influences development. Cultural and ethnic backgrounds influence almost every aspect of who we are. The values, beliefs, and history of our family deeply influence how we interpret and interact with the world. As children participate as part of cultures, they learn about interactions and relationships (Sturm, 1997). Recognizing and respecting the differences in the values and caregiving approaches of families is critical to your ability to support the development of children.

Keep an open mind and focus on what is best for children while you build relationships with families.

BUILDING RELATIONSHIPS

Attachment is the foundation of healthy relationships, and children need families to provide strong bonds of attachment. All parents and children need to form loving feelings for one another. Each parent-child dyad will approach this process differently. By being consistently warm and responsive, open to discussing differences in child-rearing practices, and allowing gradual transitions, you will nurture the parent-child relationship. Children need to feel that the culture of their parents is valued and respected. Seeing their parents treated with value and respect helps children construct a positive self-concept (Sturm, 1997). Parents also need to feel secure and competent in their role.

You can support parental decision making by listening, respecting parents' viewpoints, and helping them learn about the development of children (McBride, 1999). If you work in a multicultural program, this may be more difficult than you think. Culture impacts every aspect of communication—sometimes so subtly we fail to recognize it. Just as the culture of parents impacts their caregiving, the values, beliefs, and patterns of interaction you experienced as a child have a profound influence on your teaching practices (Sturm, 1997).

Another consideration when communicating with parents is gender. Fathers play an important role in the lives of young children, but may need additional encouragement to participate in their lives. As you plan activities and services for families, include things that are relevant to fathers such as workshops on fathering and opportunities to help in the classroom based on their abilities (Fagan, 1996). Other ways to strengthen your partnerships with families include the following:

- Make home visits before school starts, or arrange for each family and child to individually visit your classroom and meet you.

- Before the year starts, contact parents through mail or a home visit and ask them to identify their goals for their children (Pelander, 1997).

- Help parents understand your perspective and methods by starting the year with a meeting for parents about DAP. Include a presentation about the rationale for DAP, how children learn, and expected outcomes. Children can give parents a tour of the classroom and demonstrate activities (Pelander, 1997).

- Make one phone call each day, to one family in your class, just to check in and give them an update. Every month to six weeks you will have contacted all the families in your class.

- Use e-mail to update parents and make personal contact. You can send newsletter, updates on class projects, and even add extended family to the e-mail list (Ray & Shelton, 2004).

- Communicate the positives. Have children make a special phone call to parents during the day to inform parents when they have accomplished a goal or helped someone. Write notes or send e-mails to parents about the wonderful things children are accomplishing.

- Plan parent night activities. Children can share projects, put on plays, or simply show their parents around the classroom.

- Offer workshops on parent education topics. Use instructional strategies that allow parents to work in small groups and get to know each other.

- Have a parent advisory board for your school or center. Encourage parents to form committees for workshops, special events, fundraising, supporting staff, and reviewing policy.

- Communicate with one parent of each child, every week— even if it's just for a few minutes.

Table 1–46 provides further examples of professional practices that can help you build relationships and communicate with families. You may find it helpful to reflect upon your practices and set goals for improvement. However, it is often difficult for us to see our own biases. Having a peer evaluate you based on the criteria may provide additional insights and direction for growth.

TABLE 1–46 BUILDING RELATIONSHIPS WITH FAMILIES

Building Relationships with Families

Provide an example from your actual classroom practices of how you meet the following criteria.

1. All parents are welcomed and accepted.

2. Enjoyable experiences about children are shared with parents.

3. Communication routines encourage sharing information between caregiver and parent about children's schedules, general health, mood, and daily activities.

4. Sensitivity is shown for the insecurities of parents.

5. Parents and children are encouraged to develop individual "good-bye" routines.

6. The stresses that parents feel are acknowledged.

7. Parents are asked about their concerns, and services they would like.

8. Reassurance and resources are provided to help parents feel competent.

9. Appropriate caregiving is modeled for parents.

10. Programs for fathers are developed and fathers are actively involved.

11. Parent classes or support groups are provided.

12. Cultural differences and families and children are appreciated and respected.

13. Cultural differences in child/parent interactions are recognized and teacher interactions are adapted in developmentally appropriate ways to support families.

Source: Adapted from *Understanding Child Development* (7th ed.)., by R. Charlesworth, 2008, Clifton Park, NY: Thomson Delmar Learning; "Rocking and Rolling: Supporting Infants, Toddlers and Their Families. Cultivating Good Relationships with Families Can Make Hard Times Easier," by L. G. Gillespie, 2006, *Young Children, 61*(5), 53–55; and "Research in Review: Family Centered Practices," by S. L. McBride, 1999, *Young Children, 54*(3), 62–68.

SHARED DECISION MAKING

As you work with a variety of families, reconciling different viewpoints in a constructive manner will become critical to maintaining healthy relationships and a sense of community. Building partnerships with parents means being willing to share power with them through involved decision making (McBride, 1999; Sturm, 1997). At times you may struggle with meeting the demands of everyone. During such times, keep the focus on the best interest of children. Parents may have ideas about raising children that you feel are inappropriate. For instance, teachers encourage children to be as independent as possible, but in some cultures children are still spoon-fed at four and five years old (Barker & Manfredi/Petitt, 2004). The NAEYC (1996, p. 15) recommends shifting from "either/or" thinking to look beyond the short-term conflict, in order to understand the needs and goals of parents. Such situations allow teachers to be sensitive, make adaptations to expectations, and maintain developmentally and culturally appropriate practices. In this case, teachers recognized that respecting cultural practices meant they needed to change their expectations. They did this by allowing children to progress toward independence at a slower rate (Barker & Manfredi/Petitt, 2004).

Cooperative problem solving is fostered when teachers avoid the issue of right or wrong and keep the focus on what is best for children. Many times parents simply need a listening ear, accurate information, and reassurance. Barker and Manfredi/Petitt (2004) suggest the following strategies for working through differences with families:

- Acknowledge and voice to families that there are many "right" ways to raise healthy, thriving children.

- Try to understand why families do what they do. What are their goals, and how do they think about child-rearing? Acknowledge their perspective and share your own, so they can understand why you do things as you do.

- Keep your thinking flexible. Get a second opinion by discussing conflict situations and alternatives with an appropriate staff member.

To understand why families do the things they do, you will need to build your knowledge of sociocultural factors that influence them.

This knowledge, like your knowledge of child development, will become one of the most useful tools as you work with families. Sturm (1997) recommends the following discussion strategies to create an atmosphere of shared power and understanding.

- Allow parents to control the course of the discussion as much as possible.

- Ask follow-up questions about the things parents are talking about.

- Ask parents about their childhood (e.g., How were you disciplined? What things did you enjoy?).

- Share personal experiences and insights to communicate that you understand a parent's point of view.

Relationship building with children and families is the most important and potentially rewarding work you will do. Be patient, focus on building trust, communicate openly, and enjoy the fruits of your labor.

RECOMMENDED READINGS

Barker, A. C., & Manfredi/Petitt, L. A. (2004). *Relationships: The heart of quality care.* NAEYC.

Hewitt, D. (1995). *So this is normal too: Teachers and parents working out developmental issues in young children.* Redleaf Press. (ISBN 1884834078). Practical resources that address many developmental issues, including biting, aggression, fears, and separation anxiety. Includes worksheet for collaborating with parents and reproducible information on behaviors for parents.

Keyser, J. (2006). *From parents to partners.* Redleaf Press.

RECOMMENDED WEB SITES

Anti-Defamation League (ADL): http://www.adl.org. Provides information on the "World of Difference" anti-bias program for classrooms.

Center for Applied Linguistics (CAL): http://www.cal.org. CAL is comprised of a group of scholars and educators who use the findings of linguistics and related sciences to identify and address language-related problems. CAL has contributed to areas such as instruction in English as a second language, education of immigrants, bilingual education, and cross-cultural communication.

Child Welfare League of America (CWLA): http://www.cwla.org. Provides information on CWLA publications, news bulletins, conference information, and links to sites with parenting tips. It also has a link to the National Data Analysis System (NDAS), which provides information on child welfare data from individual states.

Family First Fatherhood Initiative (U.S. Department of Health and Human Services): http://www.fatherhood.org. Presents research on the importance of fathering in children's lives.

Global Children: http://www.globalchildren.org. A nonprofit organization dedicated to improving the welfare of children. Site contains information on the organization and its projects.

National Black Child Development Institute (NBCDI): http://www.nbcdi.org. Includes resources relevant to improving the lives of young African American children.

National Center for Children in Poverty: http://www.nccp.org. Provides information on children's emotional development and mental health.

Parents Action for Children (formerly "I Am Your Child"): http://www.parentsaction.org. Parents Action for Children provides parents with a platform for making their voices heard.

Women, Infants, and Children (WIC): http://www.fns.usda.gov. Presents information regarding WIC programs for pregnant women, breast-feeding women, non-breast-feeding women, infants, and young children.

PLANNING FOR DEVELOPMENT

Planning is deciding what, when, where, and how to teach. Planning is the process of connecting what you know about child development and learning and what you have learned about individual children and families with the teaching strategies and understandings that will enhance children's development. When you begin the year, most of your planning will be based on age-appropriate practices; as the year progresses you will collect information about individual children, their families, and their cultures. That information can then be used to guide your decisions about curriculum and evaluate your teaching practices.

Planning occurs both formally and informally. Expert teachers find they are planning much of the time. While driving home, shopping, or in the shower, you may think about daily experiences and mentally make adjustments. Teaching, planning, and evaluating are one continuous cycle. The most important time to plan is while interacting with children. Individualized instruction requires that teachers continually evaluate responses from students and plan adjustments. This often happens during small but meaningful personal communications as teachers listen to children, identify misconceptions, and provide thought-provoking suggestions.

Formal curriculum plans usually occur on daily, weekly, monthly, and yearly levels. Yearly plans are helpful in organizing developmental goals for the year and the most appropriate sequence to teach them. Monthly plans are important for organizing events that need several weeks of advanced preparation—field trips, visitors, projects, plays, family nights, and so on. Weekly and daily plans are usually combined on one form. These plans provide the structure that specifies what is taught, when it will happen, and how children learn. Lesson plans take many formats. You may be required to use certain planning forms, or you may be able to choose your own. Most teachers find it helpful to adapt forms to their personal teaching style. Weekly planning should include the following:

- goals (broad purpose of learning) and objectives (specific behavior or concept)
- themes, topics, or organizational concepts for the week
- needs of individual children
- ways to communicate with and involve parents
- observations and assessments to be conducted
- daily activities, materials needed, and directions
- new materials to be introduced
- field trips or visitors
- transition activities
- cleaning schedule

Despite the best planning things will frequently need to be adjusted for various reasons. Some examples include the following:

- You have the day planned for outdoor activities and there is an unexpected rainstorm. What will you do?
- It is your day off and you get a call at the last minute to cover for a coworker who is ill. You find out that nothing has been planned. What activities can you implement quickly?
- You were promised that the materials you needed for your planned art activity would be on-site when you arrived at work, but there was a shipping delay and they aren't there. What is an alternative activity you can easily set up and implement?

Being prepared at all times with a few back-up activities will make your job much less stressful. A few sample lesson plans have been provided at the end of this section for this purpose. In addition, a number of Web sites offer sample lesson plans for teachers (see "Recommended Web sites"). When downloading lesson plans from the Internet or another source, be sure each plan includes the following:

- objective or goal of the lesson
- materials needed
- directions for the activity
- appropriate age group
- developmental appropriateness

Use the planning form in Table 1–47 to create a back-up plan that you can readily use in an emergency.

SAMPLE LESSON PLANS

1. **Title:** Nutrition

   Age: 3 years and up

   Developmental Focus: Physical growth, cognitive skills, language skills

   Goal: Children will show understanding of good nutrition choices in relation to caring for their health by keeping a record of food choices.

   Materials:

   - Large paper grocery sack
   - Various foods

   Procedure: Ask the children to name things that grow. Write down their answers (older children could make their own lists). Lists might include plants, animals, and people. If you have plants or animals in your classroom, you can discuss the care they need and what happens if the animals or plants don't receive enough food and water. Discuss what plants need to grow and what animals need to grow, and then ask "What do we need to grow?"

   Write down the things children say. Guide the discussion to include nutrients. Put several types of food in a large brown grocery sack: fruits, vegetables, breads, dairy products, fats, sugars. Have a child choose one food from the sack. Discuss with the children the benefits or potential drawbacks

TABLE 1—47 LESSON PLAN

Title of Lesson or Activity:

Developmental Focus:

Goal:

Age Range:

Materials:

Procedure:

of each food. For example, cheese has calcium and helps bones grow; cookies have lots of sugar and calories, so eating too many may cause overweight. As children are choosing food, ask if they notice any foods that are similar and can be grouped together.

Guide children to group the foods into the USDA food groups (see http://www.mypyramid.gov). Finish the activity by having children plan a balanced meal for the class or their families. Follow up and involve families by having them help children record what they eat each day for a day or two, or track their diets using the USDA Web site resources.

Evaluation: Continue to discuss good food choices and periodically record daily eating habits throughout the year.

2. **Title:** Head, Shoulders, Knees, and Toes/Coordination

   Age: 4 months and up

   Developmental Focus: Motor abilities, language skills

   Goal: Children will increase their ability to recognize anatomy vocabulary. Children will increase gross motor coordination.

   Procedure: This is a simple activity that you can do almost any time, adapt to any age, and that works well in transitions or when children need to release energy. It involves using variations of the classic children's song "Head, Shoulders, Knees, and Toes." For infants, sing the song and help them move their hands to touch their head, shoulders, and so on, on model the actions for them. For toddlers, sing the song and encourage them to coordinate their actions as they name parts of their bodies. When they have mastered it on their own, add some additional body parts (neck, cheek, stomach, etc).

   Preschoolers should master this process quickly and enjoy order, wording, and speed variations. Reverse the order of the words: "toes, knees, shoulders, head." You can also do it increasingly faster or very slow, or try to do the actions with elbows instead of hands. With school-aged children this song can be used to learn the scientific names for body parts, or help them build vocabulary in other languages. They can also use it to do sit-ups by lying down on the floor to sing, then rising up to touch their toes.

   Evaluation: Teacher observation. Use a checklist of children's names to indicate mastery of the vocabulary and coordination.

3. **Title:** Patterns

Age: All ages (infants and toddlers will enjoy the repetitive wording, being read to individually, and looking at the bright pictures)

Developmental Focus: Cognitive skills, language skills

Materials:

- Book *Pattern Fish* by Harris (2000): Millbrook Press
- Paper, markers, and various art supplies for making patterns

Goal: Children will make comments that show an ability to recognize and describe patterns.

Procedure: Gather children for regularly scheduled story time. Remind them about appropriate etiquette during story time and group participation (infants and young toddlers will enjoy being read to individually). Show the children the book and ask, "What do you think this book might be about?" Acknowledge all responses, then begin reading the book. At the end of the first page, pause for a moment to allow the children to supply the predictable text that continues on the next page. After a child has done so, ask, "Matt, how did you know what would come next?" Continue reading the book. Encourage the children to describe the patterns with you and predict what comes next. Evaluate as the activity progresses. Use target vocabulary to give children feedback about their participation.

Feedback examples include the following:

"Jaxon said 'yellow, black, yellow, black,' to describe this pattern."

"Clara knew what was next; that's prediction."

"Reagan could predict what would come next because patterns repeat."

"This is a sound pattern; it describes the sounds the fish make."

Open-ended questions to ask include the following:

"How else could this pattern be described?"

"Can anyone find another pattern on this page?"

Evaluation: Teacher observation and recording of children's comments. As a small-group activity, invite the children to create their own pattern fish. You might provide various art materials that children can use to create patterns. Take pictures or make copies of the fish to document.

4. **Title:** Bear Hunt/Rhythm

   Age: All ages (infants and younger toddlers will enjoy the rhythmic chant and being read to individually)

   Developmental Focus: Language development, motor skills

   Goal: Children will use vocabulary about speed and volume of rhythm patterns.

   Materials:

   - Book *Bear Hunt* by Helen Oxenbury and Michael Rosen (2003): Aladdin (children over the age of six may not enjoy the book, but they usually love the chant)

   Procedure: Read the book to the children in a chanting rhythm. Encourage children to predict what might come next, and how they think the book will end. Children enjoy it when the author builds suspense about finding the bear.

   Increase the speed of events after finding the bear. After finishing the book, teach the children the clapping rhythm that goes with the words (slap legs and clap hand). Teach children actions to represent each part of the story. For example, when the family swims across the river, make swimming motions with your arms. Chant the story with the children while clapping. This can be done while sitting or standing (older children usually prefer to stand). Variations include "hunting" for other animals in other places. Learn about where those animals live and what types of environments would be encountered. Incorporate the new vocabulary into the chant.

   Evaluation: Teacher observation. Read the book again in a few days to see if students voluntarily express the rhythm patterns.

5. **Title:** Snow Art/Creative Expression

   Age: 2 years and up

   Developmental Focus: Social-emotional development, motor skills, cognitive skills

   Goal: Children will express positive feelings toward creating art. Children will use hand/wrist movements.

Materials:

- White glue

- Shaving cream

- Dark-colored construction paper

- Food coloring

- Plastic zipper-top sandwich bags

Procedure: Mix equal parts of glue and shaving cream (about 2 cups each). Children can help with this process. Put mixture in sandwich bags with a drop of food coloring. Help children mix colors. Clip off one corner of sandwich bag. Children make designs by squeezing mixture onto paper (much like decorating a cake). Most children enjoy the squeezing and find it an emotional outlet. Some will watch intently as they try to control how fast or slow the mixture is released. Be prepared—you will probably have to make several batches of the mixture and continually refill the children's bags.

Recruiting a volunteer to help is a good idea. The mixture takes about one day to dry. It becomes like Styrofoam when dry, opening the door for a discussion about how and why the change occurred.

Evaluation: Teacher observation. Lead a group discussion when the pictures are dry. Show each design. Encourage comments about color, texture, and lines (straight, curved, etc.)

RECOMMENDED WEB SITES

A to Z Teacher Stuff: http://www.atozteacherstuff.com. This Web site includes activities for children with special needs, as well as sign language activities.

Association for Library Services for Children (ALSC): http://www.ala.org. Includes award-winning recommended media and software for children.

DiscoverySchool.com: http://school.discovery.com. Provides innovative teaching materials for teachers, useful and enjoyable resources for students, and smart advice for parents about how to help their kids enjoy learning and excel in school.

Early Connections: Technology in Early Childhood: http://www
.netc.org. Provides information on technology and early childhood.

Education World—Internet Search Engine: http://www
.educationworld.com. Navigates 50,000 education-related sites.

Literacy Web: http://www.literacy.uconn.edu. Provides a variety of
ideas for enhancing literacy in the classroom.

PBS Teacher Source: http://www.pbs.org. This site provides a wide
variety of activity and lesson plan ideas. You can search by age,
domain, and topic.

TechLearn: http://www.techlearning.com. Tech support for teachers.
Includes reviews of software programs.

ASSESSMENT

As a teacher, one of your responsibilities will be to document the learning and development of children. Assessment of young children is the process of collecting information about the knowledge, understanding, skills, dispositions, and abilities of children. The purpose of assessment is to better understand the growth, development, and needs of children, and to evaluate the effectiveness of curriculum and programs serving young children. Accurate assessment information is critical in planning curriculum, identifying children with special needs, and evaluating programs. Currently, there is also an emphasis on standards and testing for accountability.

STANDARDS AND TESTING

Early learning standards are increasingly being used as criteria to measure the success of early education programs. *Standards* are expectations for children's learning or program effectiveness (The Council of Chief State School Officers: Early Childhood Education Assessment Consortium, 2005). Using developmentally appropriate assessment methods to measure standards is imperative. Gronlund (2006) points out that standardized tests are not effective means of assessment for young children. Young children do not understand the meaning of formal testing, and their development encompasses too wide of a range to be measured by formal testing.

As children enter school, adults often emphasize the concept of "readiness." The NAEYC (1995) released a position statement reflecting three primary concerns about the appropriateness of the concept of readiness: that young children come from diverse and unequal backgrounds that impact development; that development of young children varies greatly among individuals; and that school expectations should support diverse individual needs rather than create exclusionary boundaries. The concept of readiness implies that there are clear lines that divide developmental stages. However, development is integrated and varies in pace between individuals and across domains. For instance, a child may be cognitively advanced but emotionally unprepared for school. In such situations, the child may benefit from both the cognitive stimulation provided at school and extra social-emotional support to make a healthy transition, rather than be excluded until ready in all developmental domains.

Although paper-and-pencil standardized tests are not appropriate, they continue to be administered to children in kindergarten through third grade and are sometimes used as the sole criteria in making important decisions. These tests are based on a comparative philosophy of assessment. Norm-referenced tests are originally administered to a large group of children and then the results are used to calculate norms. These types of tests may be necessary to secure federal funding or qualify children for special programs. When children are given a norm-referenced test, the score a child receives is then compared to the established "norms." Typically, children are given a percentile ranking. If a child is in the 82nd percentile it means that 82 percent of the large group of children whose test scores were used to standardize the test scored lower than this child. When interpreting the results of standardized tests, keep in mind that the results are influenced by the values, beliefs, and language of those who formulate, administer, and take the tests. These factors influence the validity of standardized tests, and results may not report the actual capabilities of individual children.

Administering such tests to young children may increase the stress children feel, and may disrupt developmentally appropriate curriculum by pressuring teachers to teach to the test and drill and practice methods (Charlesworth, 2008). Unfortunately, the use of standardized testing for evaluating young children is a reality you will probably have to face. Common difficulties young children experience when taking these tests include difficulty sitting still, starting and stopping on time, waiting to go to the bathroom until a timed session is over, and understanding unfamiliar materials and context, as well as worry over failing. If you are required to administer standardized tests to young children, seek to make the situation as developmentally appropriate and relaxed as possible. Some suggestions include telling the children ahead of time what will be happening and telling them about any behavioral expectations that may be different than normal (e.g., they may have to stop and leave part of it unfinished). Show them the materials or let them practice answering some sample questions. Ask them if they have questions. Downplay pass/fail concerns children may have. Simply encourage them to do their best. Do not eliminate recess for more practice time. Physical activity helps children process information more efficiently. Provide parents with information about testing but advise them not to create stress by pressuring their children.

Many times this type of testing is used because of a lack of understanding of child development and appropriate assessment. The current accountability of the No Child Left Behind legislation has increased the use of standardized tests. You will have opportunities to educate parents and decision makers (principles, school boards, legislators, etc.) about the rationale for developmentally appropriate and authentic assessments, and the drawbacks of inappropriate testing. Use these opportunities to provide others with accurate information (see "Recommended Web Sites" section). You may also have opportunities to serve on committees making decisions about assessment. Best practices for teachers include a balanced approach to assessment in which many types of information are considered when evaluating the needs of children. Making decisions about placement of individual children or evaluation of teachers based solely on these tests is inappropriate. Information from standardized tests may only indicate that further examination and other forms of assessment are needed to fully determine a child's needs.

AUTHENTIC ASSESSMENT

The National Association of Early Childhood Specialists in State Departments of Education (NAECS/SDE) and the NAEYC (2002) provide recommendations for the assessment of young children. The following questions have been developed from those recommendations to use when considering an assessment tool.

- Do I fully understand what is being assessed?

- Does this assessment method accurately capture the needed information in a manner that is meaningful to young children?

- Does this assessment method include observations of children in everyday classroom activities that are conducted over a period of time and reflect growth in all domains?

- Does this assessment method consider cultural or language differences?

- Does this assessment method involve families?

- Will the information gained by using this method be useful to early childhood practitioners (including myself) and families? How?

Collecting information and documenting learning is the first step in the process of assessment. Using a variety of methods to document the learning and growth of children across all domains will give you the most complete picture of individual children. These methods include observation, parent interview, work samples (drawing, writing, sculpture, etc.), presentations, performances, photographs, and tape and video recordings (see "Assessment Ideas" section). Here are some tips for collecting information.

- Keep a positive attitude. It can feel overwhelming to track the development of a group of young children while trying to meet standards. Stay focused on developing or adapting curriculum and assessment methods to benefit young children.

- Learn to mentally collect information as you are interacting with children and watching them interact with peers and the environment. Learn to make mental notes about their development, then update children's records later that day.

- Plan for assessment. Specify observations to conduct or skills to assess each week in your lesson plan. Make assessment part of your daily routine. The more you do it the easier it will be.

- Create a system for organizing assessment documents. Use folders or binders to collect information on individual children.

- Include children in the process. Tell children you are collecting information about how they are growing and encourage them to contribute work samples.

- Always ask permission to use children's work samples. Consider making a copy or taking a picture of children's work so that they can keep the original.

- Be creative. Encourage children to work on projects, create plays or dioramas, and present their learning at family nights or to other classrooms.

- Include families in the process. Ask families to keep you updated on the accomplishments of children at home. Use paper that makes a second copy to record your observations. When appropriate, give the second copy to parents at the end of the day to update them on the progress of their children.

The next step is to evaluate what you have collected and share it with others (colleagues or families). Evaluation may take place as soon as you've completed an observation, and on a holistic scale once you've collected many forms of documentation. As you share the information with other relevant stakeholders, they will have opinions and interpretations that may surprise you. Keep an open mind. Various perspectives will deepen your understanding of children. Parent-teacher conferences are frequently used to share information with parents and hear their interpretations. Daily notes, phone calls, and newsletters are other forms of communication that may be used. As you review the information you've collected, use the following questions to evaluate.

- Does this information provide a complete picture of the child across developmental domains? If not, what information do I still need and how will I document it?

- What does this information reveal about the curriculum, the program, and me?

- Does this information indicate concerns? If so, what are they and how will I address them?

- What areas are this child's strengths? How can I build upon them?

- What concepts or activities would be challenging but achievable for this child?

- What meaning does this information have for families?

Finally, you will use assessment information to plan the next steps for children, adapt your teaching style, and make changes to the program. Not all children will be developing at the same rate or in the same way. The assessment information you gather should guide your decisions about concepts to introduce, questions to ask, and activities to encourage. Sound assessment practices will help you implement curriculum that is challenging but achievable and developmentally appropriate.

ASSESSMENT IDEAS

1. *Growth:* Go to the Center for Disease Control Web site, http://www.cdc.gov/. Under "data and statistics" you will find the percentile growth charts for boys and girls. Weigh and measure the children in your class at the beginning of the year, middle of the year, and at the end of the year. Older children can be involved in this process and enjoy collecting, recording, and graphing this data. You can plot their growth on the growth charts. Because children can gain weight, yet be falling behind in their overall growth, the percentile ranking growth charts provide another measure of continued growth.

2. *Nutrition:* Work with parents and children for one week to keep a daily record of what children eat. Evaluate food intake with them. Did they eat food from recommended food groups? Did they eat fatty or high-cholesterol foods? Did they eat foods with high levels of sugar or sodium? Use the Web site http://www.mypyramid.gov (click on "tracker") to evaluate children's food choices (some parents may be able to do this at home). Set goals with children and parents and reevaluate periodically.

3. *Physical Activity:* To evaluate the impact of physical activity and media in children's lives, provide children and families with a chart (see the "Violence" section under "Issues and Trends") to track physical activities and media viewing (television, computer or video games, Internet use) for one week. Include who is watching programs or playing the games with children and whether there is discussion about the content. Help children research information for appropriate media use. Visit the following Web sites: http://www.mediafamily.org and http://www.aap.org for further ideas (search "Media Matters Campaign"). Have children compare their personal habits to recommendations. Guide children in setting goals to balance physical activity with appropriate media viewing. Share information with families. Add tracking charts and goals to children's portfolios. Repeat the tracking chart activity and reevaluate goals every six weeks.

4. *Motor Skills:* Write children's names across the top of a piece of paper. During outdoor time or recess, write down the physical motor skills you observe each child participating in under their name. What props could you add? What structured activities could you use to introduce new skills? Are there any children who seem to have a difficult time mastering motor skills? How could you appropriately support them?

5. *Motor Skills:* Take a picture of, or videotape, motor accomplishments. If you have a digital camera for taking pictures, print two copies. Give one to the parent that day, and keep one for the child's portfolio. Write the date and the developmental task accomplished on the back.

6. *Conservation:* To evaluate children's ability to conserve solid volume, make two balls of clay the same size, then

1. Ask child if both balls of clay have the same amount or if one has more.

2. After the child agrees they are the same size, roll one into a long, skinny, snake-like shape and repeat the question.

If the child believes the snake shape has more clay, the child does not yet understand conservation of solid volume. If the child recognizes that the amount remains the same, and that only the shape has changed, the child understands conservation of solid volume (Charlesworth, 2008).

7. *Object Permanence:* To check for object permanence, try this activity with infants seven to eight months old.

Take a toy the infant is interested in, and put it down in front of the infant. Make sure the infant sees it, then partially cover the toy with a white cloth. If the infant gets the object, try again; this time be sure the infant watches you hide it completely under the cloth. If the infant removes the cloth to get the toy, object permanence is emerging (Charlesworth, 2008).

8. *Oral Language*: Assessment of language development can be done through anecdotal observations, running record observations (see "Observation" section), and video or tape recordings. When recording language samples, state the date, child's name, and age on the tape. Write a brief description of the language skills you observed. For infants, this will include cries, vocalizations, coos, babbling, imitation of words, and preverbal gestures. Repeat periodically and compare observations. For older children, note any difficulty with verbal expression, substitution and omission of

sounds, complexity of sentences, and appropriate communication of meaning.

9. *Literacy:* Literacy development can be assessed by observing how children interact with books and writing materials. Things to look for with infants and books include: mouthing, holding and opening, turning pages, pointing at pictures, and babbling while looking at the book or playing with it. Preschoolers may pretend they're reading, be able to retell stories, and write letters and names.

10. *Writing: To* track progress of writing skills, have children write and illustrate a story. Use this sample to evaluate fine motor skills and literacy knowledge. Add the book or a copy of it to the child's portfolio. Repeat this process periodically and then evaluate writing samples for similarities, differences, and signs of growth.

11. *Whole Child:* Create a portfolio to document the growth and development of each child. Include goals, developmental checklists, pictures, parent comments, written observations, artwork, likes and dislikes, funny moments, daily logs, routines, favorite songs, and so on. Encourage parents to participate in building portfolios. They may contribute pictures, anecdotal records of developmental milestones, and so forth.

12. *Humor:* To learn more about a child's sense of humor, watch for things that make the child laugh. Record these examples using the anecdotal observation method (see "Observation" section). Share information with parents and add observations to the child's portfolio.

13. *Emotional Competency:* Using the running record observation method (see "Observation" section), observe a child for about 30 minutes. Watch for indicators that the child

- is aware of his or her own emotions.

- is aware of the emotions of others.

- can manage his or her own emotions.

- can comfortably navigate social relationships.

If the child does not exhibit the ability to do these things, then identify goals and work with the child to develop emotional health.

RECOMMENDED READING

Gronlund, G. (2006). *Making early learning standards come alive: Connecting your practice to state guidelines.* Red leaf Press. Ways to meet standards in developmentally appropriate ways are explained. Tips and resources for planning and evaluation are given. Simple, practical information is presented.

RECOMMENDED WEB SITES

Council of Chief State School Officers: http://www.ccsso.org. Early Childhood Education Assessment Consortium. This organization supports states in developing assessment methods that are appropriate for children of varying cultural, language, and socio-economic backgrounds, and children with disabilities. The site includes a database of state standards, assessment methods, a glossary, and training resources.

Growing Ideas: http://www.ccids.umaine.edu. Fundamental overview of developmentally appropriate assessment; includes tip sheets.

FairTest: http://www.fairtest.org. The National Center for Fair and Open Testing. FairTest is an organization that watches over and identifies testing abuses at both the K–12 and university levels.

National Association for the Education of Young Children: http://www. naeyc.org. This organization has issued a joint position statement with the National Association of Early Childhood Specialists in State Departments of Education called "Early Learning Standards: Creating the Conditions for Success." Books, articles, and other resources are also available online.

National Institute for Early Education Research: http://www. nieer.org. This organization provides nonpartisan information based on early childhood research. It has a section on assessment and standards. Includes a database correlating state standards.

New Assessment Early Childhood Resources: http://www. newassessment.org. This site is sponsored by the University of New Mexico. It promotes innovative and appropriate assessment methods. It provides online training, conferences, printed material, and assessment tools.

No Child Left Behind (NCLB): http://www.nochildleftbehind.gov. Provides information on legislation and reports.

North Central Regional Educational Laboratory: http://www. ncrel.org. This site discusses the controversial issue of using standardized tests in early childhood.

See the "Special Needs" section for Web sites with assessment information related to specific concerns.

ISSUES AND TRENDS

BRAIN RESEARCH AND DEVELOPMENT

In the field of early childhood it is common to hear about the implications of "brain research." The reflective practitioner may wonder: "What is brain research?" "How is it conducted?" and "What does it mean in my classroom?"

Brain research in early childhood has recently grown due to advances in technology and interest from society. Specifically, nuclear medicine provides the ability to look at the brain using technology such as MRIs or PET scans. It has allowed scientists to study the brain without performing surgery (Shore, 1997). Brain researchers are neuroscientists. They study many aspects of the nervous system, including its anatomy, physiology, chemistry, and molecular biology. Neuroscientists are trying to identify how brain activity relates to learning and behavior, how the brain develops, whether there are stages of brain development, whether there are critical periods when key experiences need to occur for normal development, and how experiences affect the brain (Bransford, Brown, & Cocking, 1999). This research has greatly increased what is known about how the brain develops, and the results have emphasized the importance of early childhood. Knowledge about how the brain develops has significantly influenced what we know about how children develop and appropriate practices. We now know that (Shore, 1997):

- brain development is a complex interaction between the genetic patterns children are born with and the experiences they have.

- the brain is able to continually adapt to the environment through creating new synapses (cellular connections) and pruning (discarding) old synapses.

- early experiences, interaction, and attachment impact how cellular structures in the brain form.

- at the age of three, children's brains are twice as active as an adult's.

- brain development is not linear. There are critical periods for brain development. Different systems in the brain have different critical periods.

Critical periods of development mean that during a specific point in development, certain systems of the brain are being actively constructed on a cellular level. How this construction takes place depends on genetics and the experiences and interactions children are exposed to. If children lack appropriate stimulation, nutrition, or nurturing during critical periods, the cellular structures within the brain form weaker connections (fewer synapses). For example, during the critical periods for visual systems the infant needs appropriate visual stimulation and nutrition. If there is a significant deficit in either, visual systems may be impaired (Shore, 1997). Early childhood is also a critical time for language systems. Language abilities seem to be firmly in place by the time a child reaches age five. Language skills may be acquired later, but acquisition will be more difficult. Other systems such as emotional functioning, mathematical ability, and musical talent may develop in a more linear fashion (BrainWonders, 1998–2001c).

Synaptic connections are created in two ways. First, in the early months of life the brain overproduces synapses. As critical periods for specific systems (visual, language, etc.) emerge and close, the brain then prunes unused synapses. Second, the brain forms new synapses throughout the lifespan. The formation of new synapses is driven by experiences and learning. Both types of growth have implications for your work in early childhood (Bransford et al., 1999).

First, you can provide children with environments that present novel materials to explore, stimulate learning through problem solving, and provide opportunities for social interaction with adults and peers. This type of stimulation will strengthen existing synapses and encourage the creation of new connections. Second, you can provide a secure, responsive relationship. The brain is primarily social, and the ability for healthy cell and synapse development is strongly associated with a warm emotional climate. Third, even though early childhood may be the easiest time to build and form some neural connections, the brain has an element of plasticity and is able to adapt to environmental changes. This provides a great deal of hope for young children who have experienced early deficits. Such deficits may be tempered and even overcome through warm, nurturing relationships and appropriate supports. Finally, you can educate and encourage parents to use practices that enhance brain development. Zero to Three is an organization that provides a Web site called "BrainWonders." It has a variety of resources that are user-friendly and gives practical ideas for parents and caregivers (see "Recommended Web Sites" in the section on infants).

VIOLENCE

Exposure to violence poses significant risks to the healthy development of young children. Families are in the best position to mitigate its effects. The NAEYC (2005b) concludes that the causes of violence in American society are complex and include poverty, racism, unemployment, substance abuse, abusive or neglectful parenting, adult models of violence, wide availability of guns, and recurrent exposure to media violence (see Appendix B for signs of child maltreatment). Young children are susceptible to portrayals of violence and antisocial behavior in the media. Children are now spending more time viewing television, frequently unsupervised. Children who are consistently exposed to media violence are less likely to show empathy to those in pain and are more likely to behave aggressively. Children who witness violence may experience depression, excessive crying, low self-esteem, and fears about dying or injury (Children's Defense Fund, 2005). The AAP (2001) indentifies the following indicators that media is negatively impacting children.

- difficulty with school performance
- aggressive behavior such as hitting or pushing peers, or talking back to adults
- recurrent nightmares
- an increase in unhealthy food consumption
- smoking, drinking, or drug use

Supportive relationships with parents, positive adult role models, and a warm educational environment help children develop nonviolent coping skills (NAEYC, 2005b). Parents need sound information on the consequence of violence and the selection of appropriate media for young children. You can be an advocate for young children by encouraging families to protect them from violence. Provide a form like the one in Table 1–48 to families along with an article about the impact of media on young children (the American Academy of Pediatrics Web site offers resources and links; see "Recommended Web Sites" in the section on infants). Ask parents to watch the movies, television shows, video games, and computer games their children watch or play, and tally the number of violent, antisocial, and prosocial acts. Encourage parents to bring the sheet back for their child's portfolio, and evaluate the sheet during parent-teacher conferences.

INTERNET

As children develop greater independence and become more involved with peers, inappropriate Internet use becomes a threat. This is of great concern to present-day families. Primary-aged children are susceptible to pornography and child predators. Provide children and parents with accurate information about this issue. Some basic rules are that children should always be supervised when using computers at school, and any Internet service should have appropriate filters to protect against pornography. The Federal Bureau of Investigation (FBI, 2006) recommends teaching children the following safety precautions.

- Never give out personal information on the Internet (e.g., home address, school name, or telephone number).

- Never send a picture of yourself to someone without the permission of your parents.

- Never communicate with anyone who has made you feel uncomfortable or scared.

- Never agree to meet someone or have them visit you without the permission of your parents.

- If you read anything on the Internet that makes you feel uncomfortable, tell your parents.

- People on-line may be pretending to be someone else. A person who says that "she" is a "12-year-old girl" could really be an older man.

TABLE 1—48 MEDIA LOG

Child's name: _____   Date: _____

Name of program or game: _____   Length of time: _____

Acts of physical violence:

Antisocial behavior (name calling, teasing, making faces, etc.):

Prosocial behavior (smiling, resolving conflicts through talking, acts of kindness, etc.):

What was your child's reaction to this media?

Do you feel that viewing this media promotes healthy development for your child? Why or why not?

Providing children with accurate information and practice in making decisions (role-play) can help them make healthy decisions throughout their lives.

RECOMMENDED READINGS

Feerick, M. M., & Gerald, B. S. (Eds.). (2006). *Children exposed to violence.* Brookes Publishing Company. (ISBN 1557668043). Discusses the impact of violence in the lives of children and aspects that we may not fully understand.

Levin, D. E., & Carlson-Paige, N. (2005). *War play dilemma: What every parent and teacher needs to know.* Teachers College Press. (ISBN 080774638X). Provides strategies for resolving war play and includes practical ideas for promoting creative play.

Rice, K. F., & Groves, B. M. (2005). *Hope and healing: A caregiver's guide to helping young children affected by trauma.* Zero to Three. (ISBN 0943657938).

Sharapan, H. (2006). *What do you do with the mad you feel inside?* Family Communication Inc. Available online at http://www.naeyc.org.

RECOMMENDED WEB SITES

Center for Screen Time Awareness: http://www.tvturnoff.org. This organization sponsors a "Turn off the T.V. Week" campaign used to increase awareness of the negative impact of some media.

Federal Bureau of Investigation (FBI): http://www.fbi.gov. This government Web site provides a "field trip" and games on safety tips for children in grades K–5.

I Keep Safe: http://www.ikeepsafe.org. This is a nonprofit coalition that teaches Internet safety practices for children. Information for parents, grandparents, and educators also is provided. Curriculum training aids are available.

ISAFE Inc: http://www.isafe.org. The leader in Internet safety. This nonprofit organization provides education and resources to promote Internet safety. Includes on-line training modules for parents, educators, and students.

National Institute on Media and the Family: http://www.mediafamily.org. Provides a wealth of information on the impact of media on children and steps for adults to take.

Stop Bullying Now: Take a Stand, Lend a Hand: http://stopbullyingnow.hrsa.gov. This site is sponsored by Health Resource Services. It provides information on the prevention of bullying for children, parents, and educators. The site is designed to be user-friendly for children and is available in Spanish.

PROFESSIONAL ORGANIZATIONS

When looking to further your development, a professional organization is a great place to start. There are many national organizations, some of which have state or local affiliates.

National Association for the Education of Young Children (NAEYC)
1509 16th Street, NW
Washington, DC 20036
phone: 800-424-2460
Web site: http://www.naeyc.org
e-mail: membership@naeyc.org

Specific membership benefits:

Comprehensive Members receive all the benefits of Regular membership (described next) plus annually receive five or six books immediately after their release by the NAEYC.

Regular and Student Members receive:

- six issues of the journal *Young Children*, which includes timely articles on pertinent issues, as well as suggestions and strategies for enhancing children's learning

- reduced registration fees at NAEYC-sponsored local and national conferences and seminars

- discounted prices on hundreds of books, videos, brochures, and posters from the NAEYC's extensive catalog of materials

- access to the Members Only Web site, including links to additional resources and chat sites for communication with other professionals

National Association of Child Care Professionals (NACCP)
P.O. Box 90723
Austin, TX 78709
Phone: 800-537-1118
Web site: http://www.naccp.org

Specific membership benefits:

Management Tools of the Trade™: Your membership provides complete and *free* access (a $79 value) to these effective management tools that provide technical assistance in human resource management. In addition, members will receive the NACCP's quarterly trade journals—*Professional Connections©, Teamwork©,* and *Caring for Your Children©,*—to keep members informed of hot issues in child care. Each edition also includes a Tool of the Trade™.

National Child Care Association (NCCA)
1016 Rosser St.
Conyers, GA 30012
Phone: 800-543-7161
Web site: http://www.nccanet.org

Specific membership benefits:

- As the only recognized voice in Washington, DC, the NCCA has great influence on our legislators.

- Professional development opportunities are available.

Association for Education International (ACEI)
The Olney Professional Building
17904 Georgia Avenue, Suite 215
Olney, MD 20832
Phone: 800-423-2563 or 301-570-2122
Fax: 301-570-2212
Web site: http://www.acei.org

The ACEI is an international organization dedicated to promoting the best educational practices throughout the world.

Specific membership benefits:

- Workshops and travel/study tours abroad

- Four issues per year of the journals *Childhood Education* and *Journal of Research in Childhood Education*

- Hundreds of resources for parents and teachers, including books, pamphlets, audiotapes, and videotapes

National AfterSchool Association (NAA)
1137 Washington Street
Boston, MA 02124
Phone: 617-298-5012
Fax: 617-298-5022
Web site: http://www.naaweb.org

The NAA is a national organization dedicated to providing information, technical assistance, and resources concerning children in out-of-school programs. Members include teachers, policy makers, and administrators representing all public, private, and community-based sectors of after-school programs.

Specific member benefits:

- A subscription to the NAA journal, *School-Age Review*

- A companion membership in state affiliates

- Discounts on NAA publications and products

- Discount on NAA annual conference registration

- Opportunity to be an NAA accreditation endorser

- Public policy representatives in Washington, DC

Other organizations to contact include the following:

The Children's Defense Fund
25 E. St. NW
Washington, DC 20001
Phone: 202-628-8787
Web site: http://www.childrensdefense.org

National Association for Family Child Care
P.O. Box 10373
Des Moines, IA 50306

Phone: 800-359-3817
Web site: http://www.nafcc.org
Journal: *The National Perspective*

National Black Child Development Institute
1023 15th Ave. NW
Washington, DC 20002
Phone: 202-833-2220
Web site: http://www.nbcdi.org

National Head Start Association
1651 Prince Street
Alexandria, VA 22314
Phone: 703-739-0875
Web site: http://www.nhsa.org
Journal: *Children and Families*

International Society for the Prevention of Child Abuse and Neglect
25 W. 560 Geneva Road, Suite L2C
Carol Stream, IL 60188
Phone: 630-221-1311
Web site: http://www.ispcan.org
Journal: *Child Abuse and Neglect: The International Journal*

Council for Exceptional Children
1110 N. Glebe Road, Suite 300
Arlington, VA 22201
Phone: 888-CEC-SPED
Web site: http://www.cec.sped.org
Journal: *CEC Today*

National Association for Bilingual Education
Union Center Plaza
810 First Street, NE
Washington, DC 20002
Web site: http://www.nabe.org
Journal: *NABE Journal of Research and Practice*

International Reading Association
800 Barksdale Road
P.O. Box 8139
Newark, DE 19714
Phone: 800-336-READ

Web site: http://www.reading.org
Journal: *The Reading Teacher*

National Education Organization (NEA)
1201 16th St. NW
Washington, DC 20036
Phone: 202-833-4000
Web site: http://www.nea.org
Journals: *Works4Me* and *NEA Focus,* by online subscription

Zero to Three: National Center for Infants, Toddlers, and Families
2000 M. Street NW, Suite 200
Washington, DC 20036
Phone: 202-638-1144
Web site: http://www.zerotothree.org
Journal: *Zero to Three*

APPENDIX A: PREVENTING THE SPREAD OF DISEASE

HEALTH PRACTICES

Help children stay healthy by using sound health practices. When children enter the classroom each morning, take a moment to observe them for signs of illness. Signs of illness include: apathetic or unusual behavior, runny nose, watery or crusty eyes, coughing, sneezing, and flushed or pale complexion. Ask children how they are feeling. If you notice any symptoms, ask the parents about it. Encourage parents and children to wash their hands when entering the classroom. Parents can assist younger children with this. In addition, the following practices are recommended.

- Do not allow contagious children to attend child care settings.

- Wash your hands frequently for 20 seconds using soap and water and drying with a paper towel.

- Wash hands upon entering the classroom, before and after preparing food or feeding infants, after diapering, after wiping noses or mouths, after using the bathroom, after coughing, or any other time they may become contaminated.

- Teach and help children to wash hands after wiping noses, coughing into their hands, and toileting. Make it a class routine to wash hands before eating.

- Verify that children in your class are appropriately immunized.

- Disinfect toys that have been put in children's mouths before other children play with them.

- Disinfect all washable toys daily.

- Sanitize all feeding dishes.

- Do not use the same blankets or stuffed animals to comfort more than one child without washing them.

ILLNESS

As children arrive each day, spend a few minutes individually greeting them and talking to parents. During this time, attend to their energy level, motivation, and general appearance. Changes in activity level or facial appearance can indicate the onset of illness. Any of the following symptoms may indicate that a child has a contagious illness and needs medical attention.

- persistent cough
- fever
- vomiting
- diarrhea
- runny nose with green or yellow mucus
- rash
- is unusually sleepy or hard to awaken

RECOMMENDED WEB SITES

Fight Back: http://www.fightbac.org. Resources for education about the prevention of disease.

National Center for Infectious Disease: http://www.cdc.gov/ncidod/teachers_tools/index.htm. Provides teacher resources.

APPENDIX B: SIGNS OF CHILD MALTREATMENT

Many children continue to suffer from the ill effects of maltreatment. Child maltreatment includes neglect and physical, sexual, and emotional abuse. As an early childhood professional, you have an ethical mandate to report child abuse and neglect to the appropriate authorities in your local area. If you need help locating information, call the national hotline 1-800-4.A.CHILD. The Child Welfare Information Gateway (2006) describes the signs of maltreatment, physical abuse, neglect, sexual abuse, and emotional maltreatment shown in Tables 1–49 through 1–53.

TABLE 1–49   SIGNS OF MALTREATMENT

Signs of Maltreatment

- Child has learning problems (or difficulty concentrating) that cannot be attributed to specific physical or psychological causes.
- Child is watchful—seems to be waiting for something bad to happen.
- Child shows sudden changes in behavior.
- Child is overly passive, compliant, withdrawn, or aggressive.
- Child arrives early, stays late, and does not want to go home.
- Medical treatment for injuries is not sought.
- Parents seem unconcerned about child.
- Parent denies or blames difficulties on others.
- Parent asks teacher to use harsh discipline methods.
- Parent appears to view the child as bad, worthless, or burdensome.
- Parental expectations exceed child's ability.
- Parent seems to need child to attend to and satisfy their emotional needs.
- Parent and child rarely touch or look at each other.

(Continued)

TABLE 1–49   SIGNS OF MALTREATMENT (*Continued*)

Signs of Maltreatment

- Parent and child consider their relationship in a completely negative light.
- Parent and child state that they do not like each other.

Source: Adapted from *Signs of Child Abuse and Neglect.* Child Welfare Information Gateway. Available online at http://www.childwelfare.gov/pubs/factsheets.cfm

TABLE 1–50   SIGNS OF PHYSICAL ABUSE

- Child has unexplained burns, bites, bruises, broken bones, or black eyes.
- Child has bruises or other marks noticeable after an absence from school.
- Child appears frightened of the parents and cries or does not want to go home.
- When adults approach, child shrinks or shys away.
- Child reports an injury by an adult, including caregivers or parents.
- Parent gives conflicting, unconvincing, or no explanation for the child's injury.
- Parent refers to the child as "evil," or in a very negative way.
- Parent uses harsh physical discipline with the child.
- Parent has been abused as a child.

Source: Adapted from *Signs of Child Abuse and Neglect.* Child Welfare Information Gateway. Available online at http://www.childwelfare.gov/pubs/factsheets.cfm

TABLE 1–51   SIGNS OF NEGLECT

Signs of Neglect

- Child is consistently or frequently absent from school.
- Child begs or steals food or money.
- Child is not receiving medical or dental care, immunizations, or glasses.
- Child is consistently dirty and has severe body odor.
- Child does not have appropriate clothing for the weather.
- Child abuses alcohol or other drugs.
- Child states that there is no one at home to provide care.
- Parent appears indifferent toward the child.
- Parent seems apathetic or depressed.
- Parent acts irrationally or in a bizarre manner.
- Parent abuses alcohol or other drugs.

Source: Adapted from *Signs of Child Abuse and Neglect.* Child Welfare Information Gateway. Available online at http://www.childwelfare.gov/pubs/factsheets.cfm

TABLE 1–52   SIGNS OF SEXUAL ABUSE

Signs of Sexual Abuse

- Child displays difficulty walking or sitting.
- Child suddenly refuses to change for gym or to participate in physical activities.
- Child reports nightmares or bed-wetting.
- Child experiences a sudden change in appetite.
- Child has bizarre, sophisticated, or unusual sexual knowledge or behavior.
- Child is pregnant or contracts a venereal disease, particularly if under age 14.
- Child runs away.
- Child reports sexual abuse by an adult, caregiver, or parent.
- Parent strictly limits the child's contact with other children, especially of the opposite sex, and is unnecessarily protective of the child.
- Parent seems secretive and isolated.

Source: Adapted from *Signs of Child Abuse and Neglect.* Child Welfare Information Gateway. Available online at http://www.childwelfare.gov/pubs/factsheets.cfm

TABLE 1–53   SIGNS OF EMOTIONAL MALTREATMENT

Signs of Emotional Maltreatment

- Child shows extremes in behavior—overly compliant or demanding behavior, extremely passive or aggressive behavior.
- Child displays behaviors that are inappropriately adult (e.g., parenting other children) or inappropriately infantile (e.g., frequently rocking or head-banging).
- Child is delayed in physical or emotional development.
- Child has attempted suicide.
- Child reports feeling a lack of attachment to the parent.
- Parent constantly blames, belittles, or berates the child.
- Parent will not consider offers of help for the child's problems or seems unconcerned.
- Parent overtly rejects the child.

Source: Adapted from *Signs of Child Abuse and Neglect.* Child Welfare Information Gateway. Available online at http://www.childwelfare.gov/pubs/factsheets.cfm

RECOMMENDED WEB SITE

Child Welfare Information Gateway: http://www.childwelfare.gov. Training resources and information about signs and symptoms of child maltreatment.

APPENDIX C: REFERENCES

Allen, K. D., & Marotz, L. R. (2007). *Developmental profiles: Prebirth through twelve* (5th ed.). Clifton Park, NY: Thomson Delmar Learning.

Allington, R. L. (2002). What I've learned about effective reading instruction from a decade of studying exemplary elementary classroom teachers. *Phi Delta Kappan, 83*(10), 740–747.

American Academy of Pediatrics. (2001). Children, adolescents and television. *Pediatrics, 107*(2), 423–426. Retrieved September 2, 2006, from http://aappolicy.aappublications.org; 107/2/423.

American Academy of Pediatrics. (2003). Prevention of pediatric overweight and obesity. *Pediatrics, 112*(20), 424–430. Retrieved August 23, 2006, from http://aappolicy.aappublications.org

American Academy of Pediatrics. (2005a). Sleep issues. Retrieved August 4, 2006, from http://www.aap.org

American Academy of Pediatrics. (2005b). Baby bottle tooth decay. Retrieved August 29, 2006, from http://www.aap.org

American Academy of Pediatrics. (2005c). Shaken baby syndrome. Retrieved August 4, 2006, from http://www.aap.org

American Academy of Pediatrics. (2005d). Treating diaper rash. Retrieved August 4, 2006, from http://www.aap.org

American Academy of Pediatrics. (2005e). Answering your child's questions about sex: The preschool years. Retrieved August 29, 2006, from http://www.aap.org

Bainer, C., & Hale, L. (2000). From diapers to underpants. *Young Children, 55*(4), 80–83.

Balaban, N. (2006). Easing the separation process for infant, toddler families. *Young Children, 61*(6), 14–20.

Barker, A. C., & Manfredi/Petitt, L. A. (2004). *Relationships: The heart of quality care*. Washington, DC: National Association for the Education of Young Children.

Beach, S. A. (1996). "I can read my own story": Becoming literate in the primary grades. *Young Children, 52*(1), 22–27.

Bergan, D. (2001). Pretend play and young children's development. *ERIC Digest*. Champaign, IL: ERIC Clearinghouse on Elementary and Early Childhood Education. (ERIC Document Reproduction Service No. ED458045)

Berger, K. S. (2005). *The developing person: Through the lifespan* (6th ed.). New York: Worth Publishing.

Blair, C. (2003). Self-regulation and school readiness. *Eric Digest*. Champaign, IL: ERIC Clearinghouse on Elementary and Early Childhood Education. (Eric Document Reproduction Service No. ED477640)

Bodrova, E., & Leong, D. J. (1996). *Tools of the mind: The Vygotskian approach to early childhood education*. Englewood Cliffs, NJ: Merrill/Prentice Hall.

BrainWonders. (1998–2001a). BrainWonders 2–6 months old: Crying. Retrieved September 9, 2006, from http://www.zerotothree.org

BrainWonders. (1998–2001b). BrainWonders: Child care provider & FAQs. Retrieved September 9, 2006, from http://www.zerotothree.org

BrainWonders. (1998–2001c). BrainWonders: Pediatricians and family clinicians. Retrieved October 13, 2006 http://www.zerotothree.org

Bransford, J. D., Brown, A. I., & Cocking, R. R. (Eds.). (1999). *How people learn: Brain, mind, experience, and school*. National Academy of Science. Retrieved September 12, 2006, from http://newton.nap.edu

Browyn, C. (2003). Working with young English language learners: Some considerations. *ERIC Digest*. Washington, DC: ERIC Clearinghouse on Languages and Linguistics. (Eric Document Reproduction Service No. ED481690)

Buschman, L. (2002). Becoming a problem solver. *Teaching Children Mathematics, 9*(2), 98–103.

Cawfield, M. E. (1992). Velcro time: The language connection. *Young Children, 47*(4), 26–30.

Center for Disease Control and Prevention. (2005). Autism: Topic home. Retrieved August 19, 2006, from http://www.cdc.gov

Charlesworth, R. (2008). *Understanding child development* (7th ed.). Clifton Park, NY: Thomson Delmar Learning.

Child Welfare Information Gateway. (2006). Signs of child abuse and neglect. Retrieved August 19, 2006, from http://www.childwelfare.gov

Children's Defense Fund. (2005). The state of America's children 2005. Retrieved September 6, 2006, from http://www.childrensdefense.org

Chrisman, K., & Couchenour, D. (2002). *Healthy sexuality development. A guide for early childhood educators and families.* Washington, DC: National Association for the Education of Young Children.

Copple, C., & Bredekamp, S. (2006). *Basics of developmentally appropriate practices.* Washington, DC: National Association for the Education of Young Children.

Curry, N. E., & Johnson, C. N. (1991). *Beyond self esteem: Developing a genuine sense of human value.* Washington, DC: National Association for the Education of Young Children.

Da Ros, D. A., & Kovach, B. A. (1998). Assisting toddlers and caregivers during conflict resolutions: Interactions that promote socialization. *Childhood Education, 75,* 25–30.

Damon, W. (1988). *The moral child: Nurturing children's natural moral growth.* New York: The Free Press.

Early Connections: Technology in Early Childhood Education. (2006). Selecting software for young children. Retrieved November 9, 2006, from http://www.netc.org

Fagan, J. (1996). Principles for developing male involvement programs in early childhood settings: A personal experience. *Young Children, 51*(4), 64–71.

Federal Bureau of Investigation. (2006). Internet safety. Retrieved August 6, 2006, from http://www.fbi.gov

Fogel, A. (2001). *Infancy: Infant, family, and society* (4th ed.). Belmont, CA: Wadsworth.

Gallagher, K. C., & Mayer, K. (2006). Teacher-child relationships at the forefront of effective practice. *Young Children, 61*(6), 44–49.

Gillespie, L. G. (2006). Rocking and rolling: Supporting infants, toddlers, and their families. Cultivating good relationships with families can make hard times easier! *Young Children, 61*(4), 53–55.

Gillespie, L. G., & Seibel, N. L. (2006). Self-regulation: A cornerstone of early childhood development. *Young Children, 61*(4), 34–39.

Gronlund, G. (2006). *Making early learning standards come alive: Connecting your practice to state guidelines.* St. Paul, MN: Redleaf Press.

Hart, C. H., McGee, L. H., & Hernandez, S. (1993). Themes in peer relationships literature: Correspondence to outdoor peer interactions portrayed in children's storybooks. In C. H. Hart (Ed.), *Children on playgrounds: Research perspectives and applications* (pp. 371–416). Albany, NY: SUNY Press.

Helm, J. H., & Katz, L. (2001). *Young investigators: The project approach in the early years.* New York: Teachers College Press and National Association for the Education of Young Children.

Herr, J., & Swim, T. (1998). *Creative resources for infants and toddlers.* Albany, NY: Delmar Learning.

International Reading Association & the National Association for the Education of Young Children. (1999). *Learning to read and write: Developmentally appropriate practices for young children.* Washington, DC: National Association for the Education for Young Children.

Katz, L., & Schery, T. K. (2006). Including children with hearing loss in early childhood programs. *Young Children, 61*(1), 86–95.

Malouff, J. (2002–2004). What if a lion won't roar: Ways teachers can help students overcome shyness. Retrieved September 4, 2006, from http://www.une.edu

Marcon, R. A. (2003). Research in review. Growing children: The physical side of development. *Young Children, 58*(1), 80–87.

Marion, M. (2002). *Guidance of young children* (6th ed.). New York: Prentice Hall.

Marotz, L. R., Cross, M. Z., & Rush, J. M. (2005). *Health, safety, and nutrition for the young child* (6th ed.). Clifton Park, NY: Thomson Delmar Learning.

McBride, S. L. (1999). Research in review: Family centered practice. *Young Children, 54*(3), 62–68.

McGee, L. M., & Richgel, D. J. (2004). *Literacy's beginnings: Supporting young readers and writers.* Boston: Allyn & Bacon.

McLaughlin, B. (1992). Educational practice report: 5 myths and misconceptions about second language learning: What every teacher needs to unlearn. *Educational Practice Report, 5.* National Center for Research on Cultural Diversity and Second Language Learning. Retrieved November 25, 2006, from http://www.ncela.gwu.edu

Mulligan, S. A. (2003). Assistive technology: Supporting the participation of children with disabilities. *Young Children, 58*(6), 50–51.

National Association for the Education of Young Children. (1995). School readiness: A position statement of the National Association for the Education of Young Children. Retrieved October 27, 2006, from http://www.naeyc.org

National Association for the Education of Young Children. (1996). *Position statement. Developmentally appropriate practice in early childhood programs serving children from birth through age 8.* Washington, DC: Author. Available online at http://www.naeyc.org

National Association for the Education of Young Children. (2005a). *Code of ethical conduct and statement of commitment.* Washington, DC: Author. Available online at http://www.naeyc.org

National Association for the Education of Young Children. (2005b). NAEYC position statement: Violence in the lives of young children. Retrieved August 30, 2006, from http://www.naeyc.org

National Association for Gifted Children. (2005). What is gifted? Retrieved August 26, 2006, from http://www.nagc.org

National Association for Sport and Physical Education. (2006). Recess for elementary school students. Retrieved September 2, 2006, from http://www.aahperd.org

National Association of Early Childhood Specialists in State Departments of Education & National Association for the Education of Young Children. (2002). Early learning standards: Creating the conditions for success. Retrieved September 4, 2006, from http://www.naeyc.org

National Center for Research on Cultural Diversity and Second Language Learning. (1995, October). Fostering second language development in young children. *Online Resource Digest,* Center for Applied Linguistics. Retrieved November 25, 2006, from http://www.cal.org

National Dissemination Center for Children with Disabilities. (2004a). Downs syndrome. Retrieved November 25, 2006, from http://www.nichcy.org

National Dissemination Center for Children with Disabilities. (2004b). Learning disabilities. Retrieved November 25, 2006, from http://www.nichcy.org

National Dissemination Center for Children with Disabilities. (2004c). Speech and language impairments. Retrieved November 25, 2006, from http://www.nichcy.org

National Education Association. (2006). Classroom meetings: A democratic approach to classroom management. Retrieved September 2, 2006, from http://www.nea.org

National Institute of Mental Health. (2006a). Attention deficit hyperactivity disorder. Retrieved September 2, 2006, from http://www.nimh.nih.gov

National Institute of Mental Health. (2006b). Treatment of children with mental disorders. Retrieved November 11, 2006, from http://www.nimh.nih.gov

National Institute of Mental Health. (2006c). Shy temperament: More than just fearful. Retrieved November 11, 2006, from http://www.nimh.nih.gov

National Institute on Drug Abuse. (2006). Preventing drug abuse among children and adolescents: Prevention principles. Retrieved September 4, 2006, from http://www.drugabuse.gov

Owocki, G. (2001). *Make way for literacy*. Portsmouth, NH: Heinemann.

Pelander, J. (1997). My transition from conventional to more developmentally appropriate practices in the primary grades. *Young Children, 52*(7), 19–25.

Piaget, J., & Inhelder, B. (1969). *The psychology of the child*. USA: Basic Books Inc.

Pica, R. (1997). Beyond physical development: Why young children need to move. *Young Children, 52*(6), 4–11.

Quann, V., & Wien, C. A. (2006). The visable empathy of infants and toddlers. *Young Children, 61*(4), 22–29.

Ray, J. A., & Shelton, D. (2004). Connecting with families through technology. *Young Children 59*(3), 30–32.

Riblatt, S. N., Obegi, A. D., Hammons, B. S., Ganger, T. A., & Ganger, B. C. (2003). Parents' and child care professionals' toilet training attitudes and practices: A comparative analysis. *Journal of Research in Childhood Education, 17*(2), 133–146.

Roseberry-McKibben, C., & Brice, A. (1997–2006). Acquiring English as a second language. American Speech-Language-Hearing Association. Retrieved November 24, 2006, from http://www.asha.org

Schickedanz, J. A. (1999). *Much more than the ABC's: The early stages of reading and writing.* Washington, DC: National Association for the Education of Young Children.

Schickedanz, J. A., & Casbergue, R. M. (2004). *Writing in preschool: Learning to orchestrate meaning and marks.* Newark, DE: International Reading Association.

Segatti, L., Brown-DuPaul, J., & Keyes, T. L. (2003). Using everyday materials to promote problem solving in toddlers. *Young Children, 58*(5), 12–16.

Shore, R. (1997). *Rethinking the brain.* New York: Families and Work Institute.

Smith, K. (2002). Dancing the forest: Narrative writing through dance. *Young Children, 57*(2), 90–94.

Sturm, C. (1997). Creating parent-teacher dialogue: Intercultural communication. *Young Children, 52*(5), 34–38.

Sutterby, J. A., & Thornton, C. D. (2005). It dosen't just happen: Essential contributions from playgrounds. *Young Children, 60*(3), 26–30.

Teaching Tolerance. (1997). *Starting small: Teaching tolerance in preschool and the early* grades. Montgomery, AL: Southern Poverty Law Center.

The Council of Chief State School Officers: Early Childhood Education Assessment Consortium. (2005). Glossary: Standards. Retrieved August 15, 2006, from http://www.ccsso.org

Thomas, A., & Chess, S. (1977). *Temperament and development.* New York: Brunner/Mazel.

United States Department of Agriculture. (2003). Tips for Families. Retrieved November 23, 2006, from http://teamnutrition.usda.gov

Villa, J., & Colker, L. (2006). A personal story: Making inclusion work. *Young Children, 61*(1), 96–100.

Webb, J. T. (1994). Nurturing social emotional development of gifted children. *ERIC Digest.* Reston, VA: ERIC Clearinghouse on Disabilities and Gifted Education. (Eric Document Reproduction Service No. ED372554).

Wolery, M., & Wilbers, J. (1994). *Including children with special needs in early childhood programs.* Washington, DC: National Association for the Education of Young Children.

Young, J. C. (1997). National standards for physical education. *ERIC Digest.* Washington, DC: ERIC Clearinghouse on Teaching and Teacher Education. (Eric Document Reproduction Service No. ED406361)